Of All The People In All The World

a performance installation by Stan's Cafe

ISBN 978-1-913185-24-4

Published by Stan's Cafe
Birmingham, UK
2020

www.stanscafe.co.uk

Of All The People In All The World © Stan's Cafe 2003
Of All The Creatures Across The Globe © Stan's Cafe 2015
Everyone Born In The United Kingdom: 1947
© Stan's Cafe 2013
Small People With Big Feet © Stan's Cafe 2015
What When © Stan's Cafe 2017

Photos
Page 68 © Graeme Braidwood
Pages: 7, 9, 10, 12, 14, 45, 49, 52 © Ed Dimsdale
Pages: 23, 27, 43 © Graeme Rose
Pages: 35,36 © Karen Stafford
Pages: 16, 25 © Craig Stephens
Pages: 20, 38, 47, 65, 88, 93, 95 © Unknown
Pages: 19, 41, 55, 69, 70, 73, 76, 78, 84, 85, 87, 96, 97, 99
© James Yarker

Publication © Stan's Cafe 2020

Contents:

Human Empathy In A Granular World	2
Performances May 2003 - July 2005	7
And So It Happened	8
Factory Work	13
Performances August 2005 - June 2007	16
In The Context Of The G8 Summit	32
Performances June 2007 - August 2008	35
World Version Birmingham September 2008	44
Performances November 2008 - May 2010	53
Salisbury Cathedral sermon May 2010	57
Performances September 2010 - January 2020	62

Bonus Material

Of All The Creatures Across The Globe	85
Everyone Born in the UK: 1949	87
Small People With Big Feet	88
What When	96

Human Empathy In A Granular World:
Why seeing you laugh and cry gives me hope.

TEDx talk commissioned by Save The World - Bonn

When you grow up on a small island you keep bumping into its edges and unless you leave that island it is difficult to understand how big the world is.

I was in my late twenties when, at the wheel of a powerful van, with a credit card and passport in my pocket I landed at the port of Hamburg and first sensed the vastness of the globe. From here I imagined it was unbroken road to Vladivostock, Chennai or Durban.

We were driving to Hanover because we had just made our first hit show, it was in demand across Europe so I had started to feel like a significant artist and hence a significant person. This feeling didn't last for long. Every city we visited seemed as big and busy as the last, everyone frantically busy doing whatever they do and almost no one realised we had arrived in town to do what we do.

Back at home I reflected on my new found insignificance, I thought it may help me understand my place in the world if I understood how many people I shared the planet with. Looking up the number didn't help. 6.2 billion, what does that mean? Even written out in full the number was ungraspable.

And this I realised was the key - the number was ungraspable. I sensed that if I could gather 6.2 billion graspable things together in a room it would then be possible to take one of them away, hold that as me and look back on everyone else. Then I would understand my place in the world.

Calculations with a set of kitchen scales suggested we would need 104 tons of rice to gather together 6.2 billion grains, enough to fill four big lorries. I was shocked and disappointed because by now I desperately wanted to build this pile.

At that time, in 2003, the UK population was 60 million and so could be represented by just one ton of rice, a manageable quantity. Whilst thinking about my big rice pile I had also been reflecting on a documentary I'd heard about babies living in prison with their mothers. This led me to think about all those people whose lives I knew so little of; how many of these babies were there in prison, how many women were in prison, how many men, how does this compare to the country's population as a whole and, thinking about it, how many prison officers look after these prisoners and how many police officers chase criminals and how many judges pass sentence? I had a vision of that one big rice pile divided up into many smaller piles each carefully measured and resting on its own neatly labelled sheet of paper.

And so the performance installation *Of All The People In All The World* was conceived. Warwick Arts Centre agreed to host it, not in their gallery but in their foyer where everyone passing-by would see it, become curious and slowly be drawn in.

In that first performance we discovered this simple device of placing human population statistics side by side allowed us not just to make provocative comparisons and show changes over time but also to tell dramatic and tragic stories, to depict historic moments and even to tell jokes. Whilst we had expected people to find the installation intellectually rewarding, we were shocked at how emotional they became.

For some reason, possibly in part because of their humanoid proportions, visitors appeared to have a great sense of empathy with these grains of rice standing in for people. If a visitor found a rare stray grain of rice not resting on a sheet of paper they would bring it to us saying with concern "we've found this person, they're lost, we don't know where they belong". "Don't worry" we'd reply "we'll take care of them, they're in safe hands now, thank you for rescuing them". Our audience had bought into the rice-as-people substitution more fully that I could ever have hoped.

I was excited to note that even in vast piles the granularity of the rice remains clear, every pile is demonstrably a collection of individuals, each with their own identity, who all together form a number. And here we come to one of the key rules for the installation. We never show the numbers because the numbers get in the way; in standing in for the people numbers erase the people. In the same way that labels beside images on gallery walls compete with and distract from the images, so numbers would draw power from the rice, we don't need the numbers, we have the objects to grasp.

I was surprised when people laughed at our weak jokes - twelve grains labelled everyone who has walked on the moon beside one grain, the well known moonwalker Michael Jackson.

I was more than surprised when people admitted blinking back tears - CHILDREN WHO WILL LOSE THEIR SIGHT TODAY AND DIE WITHIN A YEAR.

Charities have long known that pictures of individuals in need create an emotional response that a number cannot replicate, but this mute disempowered parade of suffering brings its own ethical concerns.

The rice is more anonymous, it is blank and this blankness invites imaginative engagement, it becomes a screen for emotions to be projected onto.

Anonymity also allows the rice to be egalitarian. Everyone, no matter what their social status, their gender, race, age, health, fame or fortune is represented by a single, naked grain of rice.

In effect, as performers we are Gods in brown coats, we plunge our hands into the rice sacks and randomly select a grain. 'Today you will be Nelson Mandela, you will be an oligarch and you, you will be living on a landfill site in Rio De Janeiro'. We are made of the same substance, we are all of equal worth and here in this room, under this same light, glowing golden, visitors will see us as such and recognise this to be true.

Within two years of its first presentation *Of All The People In All The World* came to Germany - we were back - this time in a tram shed in Stuttgart with a lot of rice, four lorry loads, 104 tons, we'd built a map of the world, a map measuring out human circumstance and endeavour, folly and triumph, celebration, tragedy and disgrace on a granular level, at the scale 1 to 1, a map as big as the territory.

This moment had a profound impact on me. If you ever need a humbling experience try holding one grain of rice in the palm of your hand whilst surrounded by 6.2 billion other grains.

This was in 2005 and since then the installation has toured to galleries and theatres, tents, shop units, cathedrals, community halls, a gymnasium and museums. Everywhere it goes it is re-made anew with fresh statistics for that new time, in that new place, for and with new people with new histories and everywhere we go these people bring me new hope because everywhere we take the rice we find people who share a fascination with the world, their place in it and the people they share it with.

Around the world people are shocked by the same provocative comparisons The World's Dollar Millionaires beside The World's Refugees, shocked by the scale of us, The Population of China, The Population of India, shocked by our economics McDonalds Customers Today Worldwide, employees of Walmart, everyone working for less than $2 per day. Everywhere we go people display the ability to leap into the lives of others and empathise with them.

It gives me hope that a human being can show enough compassion for a grain of rice that they will pick it up from the floor and try to find it a safe home. If we can show this much concern for a grain of rice representing a person how much more concern must we be capable of displaying for an actual person?

Knowledge is crucial and empathy powerful and our show delivers both of these but even combined they are not enough. How do those of us who seek to bequeath a better world to those who follow us, convert this knowledge and empathy into action, into change?

Ultimately it is so much easier to take responsibility for a grain of rice than the human it represents. It is safe for us to pluck a grain of rice from the floor, this costs us nothing, but to pluck someone from a leaky boat on the Mediterranean is to take on a much more open ended, costly and complicated responsibility.

It is easy to be shocked at the growth of the number of airline passengers over time, or the number of people displaced by flooding in Bangladesh, or people made homeless by other extreme weather events, or facing water rationing in Cape Town, or fighting wildfires in the United States. It is all very well to take a deep breath when you see counted out the thousand plus citizens of Chad who together each year generate only the same carbon emissions as you or me.

It is easy to be shocked and empathetic but at what point does this shock and empathy ignite and transform into action? This ignition point is difficult to reach, especially if any action threatens to result in our lives becoming even slightly less luxurious than they currently are and if we don't recognise anyone else making even these small sacrifices it is easy to think "why should I?" or "what's the point?" Well, the point is to lead by example, to show it's possible, to be a trend setter. The challenge is not to be a hypocrite, to say one thing and do another, to have good intentions and never follow through. Am I optimistic?

Yes, because to be less than hopeful is to accept defeat and because every day I see human empathy displayed in our granular world and watching you laugh and cry, this gives me hope.

James Yarker, 17th November, 2018

Warwick Arts Centre, Coventry
12th - 15th May, 2003

"What does the population of Coventry look like measured out in rice? A team of enigmatic auditors arrive at Warwick with 674Kg of rice, a grain for everyone in the country. Over four days they carefully measure out a series of statistics: everyone born today, everyone who died in the Holocaust, all the millionaires in the country, everyone who is HIV positive"

Brochure copy.

Birmingham Cathedral
7th - 10th October, 2003

Merry Hill Shopping Centre, Dudley
February 2004

Members of Dudley Borough Council's Marketing Team had seen victims of the Holocaust weighed out in rice in our Birmingham Cathedral show. They asked if we would put it in the window of a touring Anne Frank exhibition that was coming to vacant shop unit.

Excited by the chance to explore our show in a new way we agreed. We mixed World War II statistics with local interest stories. The display provoked huge interest with crowds three deep pushing up against the glass. They say over 30,000 people visited the show in just four weeks.

Leeds Metropolitan University
16th - 19th May, 2005

Annie Lloyd had seen the show in Birmingham Cathedral and wanted the Studio Theatre to present it in Leeds. Although we had wanted to include Leeds as part of a UK tour in the autumn, a citywide festival, Art In The Public Realm, meant the spring dates were too good to resist.

With the World Version in Stuttgart looming this performance was a chance to introduce two new performers to the show and for Karen Stafford, our newly appointed Production Manager, to see the show in action.

Although the foyer space outside the University Library was very small, this restriction was a good discipline and more than offset by the show's great visibility and high audience numbers. With people passing by each day we were also encouraged to make regular changes to the layout and to respond to audience suggestions.

Theater Der Welt, Wagenhalle, Stuttgart
20th June - 10th July, 2005

Essay: And So It Happened.
And so it happened and, eerily, went roughly to plan. Instead of rehearsals we had planning. From the angles of loose rice at rest we calculated volumes and floor prints. We established how many millions would sit per metre on our wide rolls of paper; how much paper we would need of what size; how many forklift days we'd need and how many performers for how long; how many bags in which piles and how many would remain unopened at the end?

With a scale plan of the Wagenhalle and cut-outs for the rice features, we sketched in flimsy paper what would become hours of back-break. We had only ever seen the hall piled high as a Flohmarkt; now, empty, it took our breath away. Too big to compete with, too full of character to ignore, we had to collaborate with the building. The monumental steel topped table we found there became the centrepiece, the crane it's backdrop and inspection steps a twist. A metallic floor and soot on the wall suggested coal mining, Chernobyl and a business zone. Crash barriers provoked motor racing. FBI special agents hid beneath a grill. Fire extinguishers obviously induced fire statistics. The smart area of tiled floor inspired the grandiose arc of the world's governments. Wood covered inspection pits became paths through the landscape. For those with an acute eye two spatial logics could be seen at play, thematic zoning overlay a more familiar pattern.

Initially we had thought we would build up with small statistics from the entrance door and place China to round them off before the rest of the hall come into view. Yet, as we pushed pieces of paper around on our diagram back in Birmingham, a new logic emerged. The proportions of the building started to suggest a map set out in Mercator's classic projection with the Entrance and North America top left, Exit and New Zealand bottom right. In accordance with the map top right is the vastness of the Chinese population now echoed in the bottom left by the world's population at three points in history. This stomach turning triptych was placed in a slightly walled-off zone perhaps suggesting it's historic status. As is the way with these things, after the event it became difficult to imagine we ever contemplated any other logic.

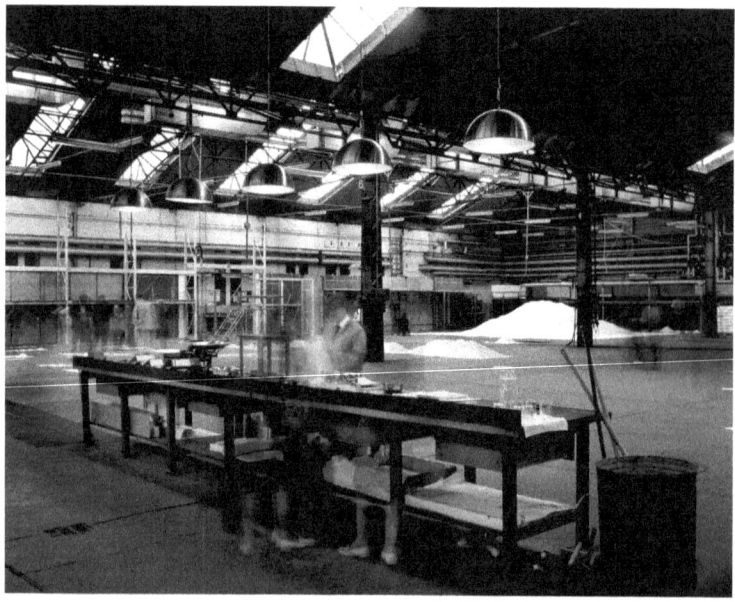

We kept the central isle clear to give the installation space to breath. We knew the hills would act visually as landmasses and if these were landmasses then the floor between must become oceans, so we floated A4 vessels on the concrete.

A major challenge came converting our fluid UK show, with its emphasis on compression and witty lateral thinking, into this huge global version. As befits a big beast, the Stuttgart show had a more measured, and powerful tread. Whole countries could now be placed side by side. Exhaustive inventories were possible, even required. Still we tried to present a mix of ideas to keep surprises and interest bubbling. We looked to mix global issues with local references. To balance large numbers representing major historic events we showed small domestic numbers. We wanted jokes along with the shocking. We became interested in scenes conjured by text describing a place, time and action represented by rice. In order to stop the Wagenhalle becoming a graveyard of official statistics, often about death, we scoured papers for less official numbers and hit the streets to record unofficial statistics.

By 18th June there were over a thousand statistics set out. The opening night was full of emotion. It was wonderful to see a large crowd sprinkled with faces familiar from our research workshops. I was too tense to be with the show in its opening hour, but later wandered in to find people engrossed, it seemed all would be all right. That night we celebrated into the night in our Green Room and emerged to find the rice glowing in moonlight, the table and globe spot-lit, seemingly miles apart. Systemnet threw its ghostly voices around the void. We caught our breath and vowed to stage a torchlight version.

So started three weeks of performance that doubled as work. Our fantastic local performers laboured in an amazingly dedicated fashion. Cleaning, translating, thinking and creating. They needed to be precise and concentrated, often in very hot conditions. Placing golden rice on crisp white paper in a dirty industrial building looked fantastic but with thousands of visitors each week maintenance duties were constant.

The show continued to develop, responding to the interests of its visitors and performers. Current affairs played their part and people started to place themselves in the landscape. The Wagenhalle leaked in heavy rain so each day was extended by covering key points in plastic at night and unveiling them in the morning. As enormous storms hit us even these covers were not enough, flooding swept away the tsunami victims amongst others, performers worked franticly to save China whilst in the real world thousands lost their homes there. With trouser legs rolled up we asked; is the metaphor growing too strong?

Slowly people talked to people and word got around. Early visitors returned recommending others. Reviews started to work their work. Finally people realised they were running out of time and could put it off no longer. The last days became a frenzy. On 10th July over a thousand people came to visit. Watching the last stragglers leave on that last day was a strange and hollow event – the end somehow not just of a show, but of an era.

Performing the World Version of this show was always our big dream; that it happened bearly two years after the idea's first staging seems little more than miraculous. It now looks as if the show will have a long and varied life, it even seems more world versions will be staged. Whatever happens it is difficult to image that this first version, made for Theatre Der Welt, with the people of Stuttgart, will ever be anything less than definitive.

James Yarker, September 2005

Essay: Factory Work.
Back-ache and 25g rice sacks. When I met James in Birmingham before flying to Stuttgart I had forgotten to factor in the need for a rigorous personal fitness regime.

The population of the world expressed through 104 tons of Italian rice fitted into four twelve wheeler trucks. These were easily dwarfed by the location for *Of All The People In All The World*. The Wagenhalle, a beautiful turn of the century build, a former tram depot, arms factory and bus repair garage is vast. Karen, James and the get-in team set to with their strategy for moving rice sacks into position. Dimensions of white paper were measured, optimum angles of rice sack gradient were calculated and forklift trucks revved into action. Chalk marks were drawn on the floor and whole subject regions, continents and eras were mapped across the space. I forgot to warm up.

On Day Two of a ten day get in I felt exhausted after completing the first statistic, a grain of rice for every Brazilian Catholic. It was good to get involved directly in working with the rice instead of watching the rest of the team speaking knowledgeably about the final shape of the show. The mapping of the performance in these first three days established a really solid deadline for all of us and I felt fired up to play my part in building the show.

In the hot afternoon of Day Five I walked with James to look at the three rice mounds representing the world's population pre-1901. Sunlight pouring through the Wagenhalle's louvred windows cast cloud shadows across these largest of rice mountains. We stood in silence and watched the light change subtly. The show was nowhere near ready to open but there was a real satisfaction in being close to these structures. I knew how much work had gone into making them and I enjoyed their stillness.

I gradually settled into a routine based around specific tasks of measuring, weighing and cleaning. These all required physical effort and concentration. What I found tricky from the start was switching between the repetitive mechanical action of moving rice and the precision needed to make the rice fit into the narrative James was looking for.

The fresh performers arriving from the UK and our German team colleagues found my grim faced determination a bit wearing and I'm not surprised. Working on this show for five weeks made me reflect on my ability to work with others in a close team. Whilst I could listen and follow instructions it took me the first week to understand the value of balancing a need to get the show into shape with including team members in the rationale for what they were doing. It's easy to avoid explaining your thinking when you are hauling rice all day.

The get-in and early period of performance surprised me as team members found their preferred working method and special interests very quickly. It became apparent within a few days of the opening; who preferred research to physically shaping the show. The all rounder award had to go to Sarah

Archdeacon for managing to maintain a clear performance mode, research relevant statistics and shape her allotted area of the Wagenhalle without losing her mind completely.

Obvious challenges to our collective morale came with Stuttgart's heatwave and violent storms. Soaring temperatures alternated with near disastrous flooding, which strangely seemed to reinvigorate the team and inspire them to make the show look better than it did pre-deluge. Despite the griping and shuffling which accompanies any run of a performance the team adopted a factory worker attitude to running the show. Petty hierarchies, practical jokes, surreptitious bullying and flirtation kept each shift on track with Tannoy announcements and the 6 o'clock chimes regulating our working day. Whilst I enjoyed the company of my fellow workers I found quiet time cutting paper with our guillotine. Hidden from the main floor of the show it gave me a chance to think and be mindful of a single focussed task.

Beyond the routine work of maintaining the show I met people who were pleased to tell me their stories and contribute their personal statistics to the landscape. I won't forget the Physics professor who returned for the third time on the busiest day of the show. His story poured out in the last fifteen minutes of the final day. His personal statistic appeared in the Stuttgart zone of the performance. Three grains of rice on A4 sheet of white paper: his mother, himself and his younger brother. All had fled from the advance of the Red Army across Germany in the winter of 1944. They had hidden in a farmhouse and been fed and sheltered by the farmer. The little brother was only a week old and needed milk to survive. The professor described cramped freezing trains, a frightened mother and a father lost on the Eastern Front. The family had survived and eventually been reunited in Stuttgart. I liked the stories which made sense of being in this city with this show. When it came to leaving the on the last evening I walked the space in near darkness. The Wagenhalle hosted us for five weeks, it lent us its factory heat, dirt and elegant design, space in which to build a unique event.

Mike Kirchner, September 2005

Edinburgh College of Art
22ⁿᵈ - 25ᵗʰ August, 2005

Wunder der Prairie Festival, Mannheim
15ᵗʰ - 17ᵗʰ September, 2005

Here the last night coincided with election night and for the first time the show elicited applause as grains of rice representing victorious candidates were added to the appropriate political party pile.

Emily Carr Institute, Vancouver
3ʳᵈ - 18ᵗʰ October, 2005

Worcester Cathedral
12ᵗʰ - 15ᵗʰ October, 2005

NOW Festival, Nottingham
17ᵗʰ - 20ᵗʰ October, 2005

Warwick Arts Centre, Coventry
25ᵗʰ - 29ᵗʰ October, 2005

Festival Escena Contemporanea, Madrid
6th - 7th February, 2006

Blog Post: Rice in Madrid
Of All The People In All The World: Europe opened at the Chamartin Railway Station, Madrid on Monday. This is the first time the show has been staged on this middle scale and I think it's a great size. There is enough rice to put out some impressive statistics and these larger piles help give the piece a strong sculptural feel. At the same time, twelve tons of rice is far more manageable than the hundred and four tons the world scale [currently] entails.

Our Madrid venue is impressive, it has a contemporary barrelled roof, decent natural light and the smooth tiled floor is ideal. Each time we take the show out we learn something new about it. Here the rice arrived in ten enormous sacks rather than the 20 or 25kg bags we are familiar with. This made the get-in far more laborious than usual but a set of industrial scales, willing local help and an impressively committed Stan's team meant we opened on time.

The whole business of weighing out rice gets a bit obsessive after a while, especially when you're spending hours just filling up 20kg bags. I've had to go cold turkey, flying home to try and set up some fresh projects for the next few years, whilst the rest of the team stay on.

Hopefully Amanda, Charlotte G, Heather, Jake and Karen will get to see some of the local sights, The Prado and a show or two from the festival before they close at the end of the week and the whole enterprise rolls on to Valencia.

James Yarker, 8th February, 2006

Festival VEO, Valencia
17th - 25th February, 2005

Manchester City Art Gallery
2nd - 5th March, 2006

Fabbrica del Vapore, Milan
28th May - 1st June, 2006

World Summit on Arts and Culture, Newcastle
13th - 18th June, 2006

Email home: Newcastle Gateshead 17th June 2006
[…] I am at the World Summit for Arts and Culture in Newcastle Gateshead, with the rice. […] People are continually surprised and amused. Kids perception of themselves in the world is challenged. One girl sat for quite a while looking at the mountain of hungry children in the world, another looked at me excitedly and said "it's like the moon" another wanted to jump into the population of Iraq, someone's mum had been to Hong Kong and got food poisoning. Another said there can't only be 3 people per KM squared in Australia cos his aunty lives in Adelaide and there are five people in their house alone! Who is Martin Luther King? Who is Ellen Macarthur? Did your mum sign Jamie Oliver's petition?

Newcastle is a great city, welcoming and full of life. World cup fever is very much alive here, red and white everywhere you go on match days. I haven't slept through the night once since I got here, our flats are in town and more often than not it's a football chant that wakes me up in the small hours of the morning. […]

Sunday I go to Cork and we begin again, were will we start? With something Irish of course.

I hope you are all well, I'll send an update from Cork if I have time.

Much love

Heather [Burton] xxx

Midsummer Festival, Cork
21st June - 1st July, 2006

Space restrictions in the long thin Triskel Art Gallery led to a new approach to the show, clustering statistics in tight narratives designed to be read in sequence when moving round the space following a prescribed route. This allowed us some really strong combinations and stories. We learnt a lot about Irish history. Being open to a busy street meant that passers-by would pause for a look through the window and then be drawn in. This included a couple of gentlemen slightly the worse for wear, one of whom came in whilst his mate stayed outside protecting their cans of Special Brew.

Noorderzon Festival, Groningen
17th - 27th August, 2006

This great festival is centred around a park so this became the show's first outing in a tent. With interest from other outdoor festival we were keen to see if it worked. Despite torrential downpours the marquee stayed basically sound and well over a thousand people paid €4 to see a rapidly evolving array of approximately 250 statistics.

BA Festival of Science, Blackfriars Hall, Norwich
2nd - 9th September, 2006

T.B.A. Festival, Portland, Oregon
7th - 17th September, 2006

Email home: Portland 8th September, 2006
Hi all...

Short stack with bacon, eggs over easy and maple syrup, and refill coffee. America is a good land!

We arrived on Monday I think, I have totally lost track of the days. The flight was ok although the 4-hour domestic flight from Chicago to Portland was pretty hard on Robin, the two-year-old child of Craig and Charlotte, (he seems to have recovered and has recently enjoyed a reading at the library entitled "Where's Bear?" please use American accent to get the full impact).

We are staying at the Mark Spencer Hotel, easy to remember

and the rooms are fabulous, BIG bed and walk in wardrobe, it appears to be an old hotel and has a huge General Electric American fridge and a hob with all manner of buttons, and a waste disposal.... so much fun!

We came to the venue on the first morning, got our bearings and met our volunteers, Ryan and Fawn. They are very nice people and I'm sure I'll have more to tell you as the week goes on… We opened last night as part of 1st Thursday. On the 1st Thursday of the month there is a gallery open evening, there are a lot of galleries in the Pearl District where we are and we had over 300 people through. Lots of interesting people, although I felt a little sorry for a couple of kids who's dad turned the whole thing into a maths lesson […]

Portland itself is a very mad place, full of all kinds of people, with what seems to be a high level of tolerance for everyone. We've met some friendly waiters and some crazies out on the street, one guy saw Amanda and shouted" DUDE! You look like my teacher!" We also met an English man from Walthamstow singing songs with a guitar and homeless guy who told me I was the super glue that held my crying friends together.

No photos yet, I need to upload, hopefully soon.
Thanks for listening, hope you are all well

H xxx

Skirball Cultural Center, Los Angeles
26th September - 1st October, 2006

Email home: Los Angeles, 3rd October, 2006
Dear all,

So, it turns out, this place can grow on you.

[…] People here like to talk, to begin with this was really hard as their attitude seemed pretty aggressive, no-one would take the time to think about what they were looking at, they came straight to the desk "So what is this?" "Did they count all the rice?" "What are you supposed to be doing?" "Where is the performance?" "Why don't you use wild rice for the Africans?" "You should use fried rice for the people who have be executed". I'm not kidding.

I put out the 7 Million World of Warcraft online gamers to an audience of about 15, each individually asking what the pile was before I had a chance to label it. There is no waiting in the USA, TELL ME NOW!!!!

In the end it was great. 3000 people through the doors in 6 days.

Probably at least 3000 questions between the 7 of us performers, so much enthusiasm for the work, they loved it! They questioned and praised in equal measure, they challenged us to explain our motives and sources. People laughed and cried, showed us their concentration camp numbers, told us their stories of survival and immigration, enjoyed our English accents and adored little Robin.

Today was another LA adventure. We went downtown, where all the lights are bright and buildings are tall and the Mexicans and Chinese hang out. It was hot today, we quit downtown took a cab down Broadway and back to Venice Beach, Santa Monica. Amanda wanted to hire a surfboard and off we went into the ocean, I hired a boogie board. WOW! It was so much fun, the waves were big and powerful, not like Jersey where you stand around getting cold waiting for just one more wave, they kept coming one after the other. I caught a few crazy waves that came in fast onto the beach, I was flying! Amanda managed to get up to her knees, pretty impressive work.

Now I am back in the hotel thinking about packing and getting nervous about the next stop Australia. (25 days till you get there too Dan, can't wait)

Hope you are all well back home, thanks for your emails; there should be some more photos soon. Thanks for listening..

Lots of love

H xxxx

FIDENA Festival, Bochum
27th September - 3rd October, 2006

By now enough members of Stan's Cafe could perform the show for it to be presented simultaneously at more than one venue with other pieces from our portfolio performed elsewhere. Here in Bochum the show was programmed as part of a festival of 'object theatre' alongside puppet shows.

Theater Der Jungen Welt, Leipzig
4th - 8th October, 2006

Presented in a former University bookshop with huge windows looking out onto busy shopping street we felt like part of the city.

We ran workshops for schools every week day through the performance and the run culminated with young people from both Leipzig and Birmingham performing in the show together on Saturday.

Melbourne International Arts Festival
12th - 28th October, 2006

Email home: Melbourne 15th October, 2006
Hi all,

It's been a while I know. I've been here 10 days and not sent an email. Shocking behaviour. Thing is, Melbourne is a seductive city.

[…] The show opened on Thursday night as the official opening of the Melbourne International Festival. We were welcomed by Aunty Joy, whose ancestral land we are on. She performed a smoking ceremony which cleansed the air and she gave us all a leaf. There were speeches by the Deputy Mayor, and the Artistic Director of the festival Kristy Edmunds. It felt great to officially open the festival, Kristy genuinely loves the show, she said she felt that it would become the signature piece of the festival.

Now we have been open for 3 days and nearly a thousand people have been through the doors. Old and Young. They don't ask as many questions as the Americans but they are equally amazed and intrigued. 20 Million people live in Australia, nearly 1.4 billion in China. To be able to see these countries together is pretty powerful.

[…] The people here are like people at home, it's so like home it's unnerving, but the way of life is easy, nothing is really a challenge, the trams take you where you need to go and nothing is too far away. A relief after LA.

So, all is well and now there are only 2 weeks to go before Dan arrives and we can start our holiday in Melbourne. It will be gone in a blink of an eye.

I hope you are all very well and not too cold back in Blighty, Much love to you all from the other side of the world where it feels like home.

H xxxx

Letter in response to complaint: 31st January, 2009

Dear Ms Perry,

Thank you for your letter of 23rd January expressing your concerns about our performance installation *Of All The People In All The World*.

Obviously the use of a staple food product as the basis for the show was a decision we took with some care and consideration. As you have identified one of the stipulations we make when entering into a contract to perform the show is that we can be satisfied that once the show is concluded the rice finds an appropriate show. For large scale shows this generally means the rice is used between it's first and second stage washings and re-enters the food chain as normal. For other versions the rice is donated to food charities for local consumption. Melbourne was unusual for being a large version whose rice was donated in this way.

I appreciate that your concern centres on a perception that in using food to make art we are in some way undermining the value of food as nutrition, no matter what the end destination of the rice used. It is my belief, and that of the vast majority of those who promote, attend and critique the show, that it is very reverent towards the rice and its status as a foodstuff is very strong within the show. Each grain is important to the show, weighed, counted and carefully placed in context. The story of humanity told through the rice heightens our awareness of the world, its triumphs and challenges, world hunger included.

On balance, given the end use of the rice, the awareness raising job the show does and the overwhelmingly constructive response we have had ever since we first staged the show that it is a good and positive contribution to our world, we are comfortable with our use of rice in this context.

I enclose a few sheets from our many comments books to

emphasise that the show is sensitive and constructive rather then exploitative and uncaring.

Yours faithfully,
James Yarker, Artistic Director

Nagy Britmania Supernow Festival, Budapest
9th - 16th February, 2007

'Last October,' said our fixer, Gabor, 'people were being shot in the face with rubber bullets outside this venue. I hope that doesn't happen while you're here.'

'Yes, we hope that doesn't happen either,' we said.

With no real control over how the rice is read, we wondered if perhaps here, in a country with a complex past and equally complex present, we'd understand why the guards on our door were armed. The atmosphere was all the more heightened by people muttering to us at opening night:
'what you're doing is wonderful, but expect trouble'; to other times 'what you're doing here is an insult, I hope you get trouble'; to ultimately the most measured and representative: 'what you're doing is very interesting, and don't listen to talk of trouble, people say a lot of things.'

And that's how it went. The imposing Museum of Ethnography lent impressive space to big issues around immigration, diaspora, children's health, and the 1956 revolution, navigated via culture, transportation, and cheap gags. The cast (Hungary and its neighbours) came in 50kg 'hernia' bags, and if some were kicked over the floor, it was for the most part accidental. Besides, there was a kind of Sistine Chapel mural on the roof which drew the eye rather. An impressive array of notable Hungarians kept the narratives refreshed, and its beguiling language made seriously impressive demands on the 'insert symbol' function for the labels.

Graeme and Andy, who had been recently released from a Budapest police station when I arrived, drove back to England in The Black Maze sending us messages of support from a series of 'luxury trucker stops'. Stretched to breaking point, our translator Ildiko decided she wanted to fix toilets for a living; and Jack, Louisa, and Chris did a beautiful job of ensuring the show was the British export to be proud of (and Chris is French so fair play to her there).

Nick Walker

MASS MoCA, North Adams, Massachusetts
10th - 25th February, 2007

900 million grains of rice. A grain for everyone living in the Americas.

Sited in the small industrial town of North Adams, MASS MoCA is a contemporary art museum housed in an old factory complex. It's a huge place and people drive for hours to visit it - from neighbouring states and cities such as New York, Boston, Albany. This was our first visit to the east coast and as the MASS MoCA publicity said it was the first chance to see the show "east of the Rockies". We felt some pressure on us here (self inflicted), this being perhaps the most obviously contemporary visual art setting in which we had presented the show. That said we were actually in the theatre, stripped of its stage and seating and with its drapes pulled back revealing the original brick factory wall and windows which allowed the beautiful Massachusetts winter sunlight to stream in and choose which piles of rice to light during the day. At night the theatre lights took over, simple pools of light providing a very atmospheric and theatrical setting.

Here we also had the luxury of having Jon [Ward] with us to develop the soundtrack. He added new musical elements, some of which he composed before we arrived and some he wrote up in his little room in the bowels of the building. These new musical elements transformed the soundtrack, punctuating the show with aural moments of joy, threat, sweetness, calm and anticipation. Jon's work attracted nearly as many comments and questions as the rice. The sound now also includes moments of life in MASS MoCA captured as Jon interviewed, eavesdropped and sampled during his stay.

The show received widespread media coverage with radio interviews, photos and reviews in local press and features in the Boston Globe and New York Times. This and the marketing clearly worked - with over 5,000 visitors this was one of our busiest runs and people were very vocal in both their questioning and appreciation of the show. We had a number of repeat visits, which encouraged us to keep changing the show. It's always difficult to take things up (you become very attached to the statistics you have put out and the stories they tell) but we kept the show moving and changing, with Jake putting out his final statistic with ten minutes to go on the final day.

Email home: North Adams, 14th February, 2007
Hi Guys,
I'm sitting in the Cup and Saucer coffee shop in North Adams. It's snowing. It's been snowing for a while. There's about 8 inches of the stuff and it's still coming down. The gallery has closed, they call it a Snow Day, I'm reminded of those few days back in the early 80's when School was closed and we went sledging with the Clunes family in Rowlands Castle, it was a winter wonderland and I fell through a hedge thinking it was just snow, my wellies were full of snow by the time we got home. Here a lot of the cars have snowploughs on the front but the snow is coming down so fast they can't keep the roads clear. I'm wearing my thermals as outerwear; I've run out of clothes! I'm warm but not very stylish.

[...] We've been on the radio, in all the local papers and a piece will be in the New York Times on Saturday. Everyone knows who we are in this town, they hear the English accent and ask, "Are you the rice people?"

It's sometimes very beautiful here, little white houses nestle into the mountains but this industrial town whose factory closed down in the 60's is a mix of 'beautiful old' and 'ugly decline'. It's a nice change to be taking things slowly on this Stan gig. Last year we were running around pretending to be on holiday in LA while working on the show. Here we can just have a rest, take things easy.

So, I'm off to take it easy, have a great day all.

Hx

WOMADeladie, Adelaide
9th - 11th March, 2007

Email home: Adelaide, 13th March, 2007
Hi all,

Adelaide, all done and dusted, we got there just a week ago and now Jake and me are back at Singapore airport with a few hours to kill before the final leg back to London. WOMADelaide - my first experience of a big music festival, going as an artist is the way to do it. With a back stage pass that allows you some moments of peace away from the crowds, a bar with no queue (same with the toilets) and an air-conditioned dressing room (not really a dressing room more a trailer, we shared it with a French visual arts company called Quidams, they seemed a little grumpy but their show was beautiful)

My first experience also of OATP in a tent, I started with my usual attention to detail, straight lines, carefully arranged rice, clean and neat. By the end of Sunday I had to let go to the WOMAD spirit, the tent was full of grass, ants, and people. We did our best to stop the ants making off with some individuals, (they were very persistent) I also had to ask a kid to pick up his football. Despite these extra anxieties and the incredible 100-degree heat the show was a great success with the tent constantly full of people. I spoke with a lot of people, including an aboriginal woman proud that her people were included in the Australian population stats.

From MASS MoCA to WOMADelaide a crazy few weeks of snow, sun and rice and I can't wait to be home.

Heather

Alternative G8, Mecklenburg-Worpommen, Rostock
30th May - 8th June, 2007

In The Context Of The G8 Summit
Rostock, the largest city in the north German state of Mecklenburg-Vorpommen, near the Baltic Sea, welcomed the alternative G8 summit from 5th - 7th June while the G8 took place 15 kilometres away at Heillingendamm, a selective and secluded holiday resort.

Being in Rostock with *Of All The People In All The World* gave me the opportunity to observe and try to understand what people are marching about in those big demonstrations. It also gave me the chance to witness the before and after of such events and to confirm the selective nature of the mainstream media.

Everyone knew that a big demonstration was to take place on the 2nd June in the centre of Rostock. Arriving on the 28th, I witnessed the unfolding preparation from the police. Every day more people arrived and every day more police arrived. A couple of day before the big day, our German assistant related to us that people had stocked up with food. Inhabitants of Rostock felt under siege. Anti-Riot Police made their presence very visible, all in khaki uniforms, complemented with protective gear - bullet-proof vests, helmets, guns and batons. At one point I counted 18 police vans and that was just a small portion of what was being put in place. Shop windows were being boarded up. Rumours of cash points being emptied to thwart demonstrators passed around to more confusion and unrest. The tension created by this display of force was incredible. So many police around - men, women, vans, cars, helicopters; at every corner a police presence, the unrelenting noise of hovering helicopters, the checks, the sirens.

The Big Demonstration: Saturday 2nd June, 2007
The demo started from two different locations in town, planning to meet at the harbour where the stages were ready for speeches and concerts. We arrived late due to the cancellation

of all tramways going in or out of the City Centre; bus replacements had been provided. We arrived by our venue. St-Marienkirche was a very open church, having welcomed us and our show, letting demonstrators inside for reflection and leaving its doors open for a three day prayer vigil (which, late one night, was one of the most moving moments I witnessed in my stay). We were greeted by noise, colour, vibrancy; a carnival atmosphere under the eyes of the riot police. A variety of people young, old, family, some in groups chanting, some walking on their own, lots of cameras everywhere (the police had brought theirs as well), big papier mache figures, colourful banners in many languages, all passed by us.

Different causes gathered here under the banner "Another World is Possible"; anti-capitalism chants unifying them all. The atmosphere changed suddenly when "The Black Block" passed by; young men and women wearing their uniform black jeans or trousers, branded trainers, and sweatshirts, caps; most of them hiding their face under scarves and/or sunglasses; their red and black banners forming a tight square around them, uncompromising. They were followed by more music, more colour, more vibrancy.

Later on, we heard sirens, police vans speeding to the harbour. Curiosity took the best of me, I wanted to go and see what was going on, be amongst it, to witness with my own eyes, unmediated. We were forbidden access. Police had formed a large barrier around the harbour area and stopped all those who wanted to get in. Rumours passed like a cold. Clashes had broken out between the young men and women in kaki and the young men and women in black. Stones were thrown, people injured, cars burned, arrests, water cannon and tear gas in retaliation or to calm things down. And in the middle, were all those who came there to have their peaceful say, being robbed of the attention they deserved. The burst of violence between "The Black Block" and police made the front pages. The first evening showed a fairly accurate account of the demonstration I had witnessed, but by morning the only images displayed in the 3 minute TV reports were those of the violent clashes.

Nowhere could we see or hear the joyful atmosphere that had been the main feel of the demonstration.

Over the next few days, the police presence remained. It felt very strange to be walking the streets, eating strawberries or ice cream and seeing so many police everywhere. Most disturbing for me were the constant sound reminding of their presences: helicopters over our head, sirens whizzing by. Those sirens aren't designed to impart calm.

The thing I kept thinking was that the police, those young men and women dispatched from all over Germany, were only doing their job and yet everybody resented their presence. Then my opinion changed. I needed to go to a shop that stood behind a police line. The shop front was literally 5 steps away but they did not want to let me pass. They had to stop people going up that road, "That's the order! That's the end of the matter! I stomped away, back from where I had come, entered a Shopping Centre, walked through the Chocolate and Jewellery sections and exited a minute later behind the police line and entered my destination. Their blockade was utterly inefficient. Later I realised that they did let some people go up that road after all, it became apparent that, for some reason, I was among those who had to travel the temptation route.

The Alternative G8 Summit.
I attended the closing speech of the Alternative G8 which gave me a much clearer sense of what the demonstrators were trying to achieve; basically stopping the dominance of big corporations appropriating natural resources for their profits. Vandana Shiva, the very charismatic head of the panel told us "Air, Earth and Water are resources that belong to all. They should not be privatised". I was sold on the cause and yet when I came to the speakers' table I saw they had been drinking bottles of Vittel water from disposable plastic cups. The presence of these objects undermined everything I had just heard, demonstrating the difficulty in applying those fine ideals in everyday life.

Chris Dugrenier, August 2007

The Holland Festival, Muziekgebouw, Amsterdam
11th - 24th June, 2007

All We Need, Les Soufflantes, Luxembourg
10th - 25th February, 2007 (plus six months)

Here the show was part of a larger visual art show occupying an enormous old steel works. We were to be part of the Understand zone focusing on globalisation, climate change, poverty and migration. The exhibition ran for six months so we left our installation unattended for long stretches. Our technical manager Karen Stafford returned three months in to find the show had been well cared for but felt tired and flat after a lack of updating.

Bellouard Bellwork International, Fribourg, Switzerland
28th June - 1st July, 2007

This small medieval city hosts a great international arts festival each year. Their inventive programme included a monthly T-shirt subscription and comedy Rock-Noise band AssDroids alongside us and Hotel Modern - who we bump into intermittently across Europe.

We were in a beautiful stone built arsenal alongside the old city wall and ramparts. The colour of the rice, the paper, the floor and walls all worked beautifully together, wooden pillars gave the show an interesting framing. This 8 tonnes of rice came in the 25kg bags which are standard for mainland Europe. The novelty was a pallet of useful 10kg bags, once empty of rice these started to disappear as local helpers attempted to start a new rice accessory fashion handbag. The armoury was a little small for such a magnitude of rice, as a result we concentrated on piling large statistics as high as they would go and packing them tightly together. The result was a pleasing Alpine rice-scape befitting the Swiss premiere of the show.

Le Quai, Angers
12th - 16th July, 2007 (performance)
17th July - 19th August, 2007 (exhibition)

Here the show was presented in the vast foyer space of a brand new theatre. We left the show in its finished state for a month after we finished performing. This was to be the last time we ever agreed to this arrangement. The show 'dies' if its not tended to, it is about discussion and responding to the world around it.

Blog Post: Radio Rice Calling
12th July, 2007

During the performances of *Of All The People In All The World at Theatre* Le Quai in Angers, France, the show's soundtrack *Signalnet* is gearing up a level as Jon [Ward] experiments in ambient broadcasting live from the venue. When new statistics are added to the show the performers will broadcast them on a "tannoy"; not only will this be heard in the venue but it can now be heard live online via our new station Radio Rice.

It's a great opportunity to hear how *Of All The People In All The World* grows in real time [...] Very simply, you can listen to Radio Rice live on your computer by downloading the player from www.radiorice.com or you can listen to it as a free podcast from the iTunes store. Give it try and let us know what you think.
James Yarker

Mladi Levi Festival, Ljubljana
19th - 23rd August, 2007

Metropolis Bienalle, Copenhagen
10th - 16th September ,2007

Skirball Cultural Center, Los Angeles,
29th November - 30th December, 2007

Blog Post: Freshwater Eel Declared The Winner
Progress is always slow on the first day. We try not to rush those big decisions which shape the course of the whole installation. Here part of that calculation was how to sensibly organise the piece to spread over three gallery spaces. Then we start by

placing out the big rice piles, the landmarks round which everything else is based, this too is slow work.

Day Two is always more dramatic, the medium size piles go out and small piles start to appear. Each step down in scale speeds up the placement, until the annoying territory around the 200 grain mark where numbers are too small to be confident about weighing out and become time consuming to count.

The show opens at Noon on Thursday and that looks viable. Craig has got the first gallery to an opening state with its Birth Of A Nation theme. I am lagging a bit behind in the second gallery working on a Jewish theme. Graeme spent the entire day working on three of the four massive runs of A4 sheets that will create an isle up the centre of the large Getty Gallery, linking [a pile showing] the Population of Brazil with [a pile showing] the Population of the USA and somehow he has kept his sanity. Jake, aided in varying measure by Jo, Charlotte and Robin, was prolific knocking out medium size piles in the main gallery. As ever Karen discreetly prodded and prompted venue staff to sort out sound and power and internet access and tables and so on, whist simultaneously label printing the dozens of labels everyone except I required.

I was slow on the label front not least because the show's publicity push continued with a trip to KPFK. I was gate-crashing Yatrika Shah-Rais' Global Village programme, interrupting her seductive flow of World Music tunes to plug the rice. Yatrika had met our Chair, Alan James at a World Music Conference, had seen the show at Skirball last year and programmes music at the venue too, so it was friendly territory. Normally doing radio interviews I'm overwhelmed by the question 'Who's Listening?' which mutates into the question 'Is Anyone Listening?' So when Yatrika played a Youssou N'Dour track, plugged his forthcoming gig at UCLA and offered four free CDs to the first four listeners to call in, it was gratifying to see the green call waiting buttons on the studio phone light up and in a steady sequence – one to ten. People were listening, the crucial question is of course then the third classic radio interview question: 'Will Anyone Have Any Interest In What I'm Saying?' At the close of the interview Yatrika mentions Free Tickets To The Show and all eyes turn to the phone, there's an awful pause and then yes, one, two, pause, three, four, five, pause yes Full House ten flashing buttons. Mr. N'Dour can rightly claim to beat us for speed of response and we may have only had ten calls total but we lit the lights and punched the air.

We stayed on [in the gallery] till a bit gone seven just adding this pile, just adding that pile. Back at base Jo, Charlotte and Robin were watching *The Simpsons* on a television the size of a pool table. With various strategies being adopted for dinner Graeme and I walked to a local All You Can Eat – Sushi restaurant. We didn't eat all we could, but we ate all we wanted, which allowed us to conduct a fairly comprehensive tasting of all that the menu had to offer. Freshwater Eel was declared the winner.

The day spiked between homesickness and joy and laughter and pride and rounded off rather wonderfully with a blog entry from the anonymous donor who made this whole fantastic return trip possible.

James Yarker

Blog Post (Skirball): And now, a word from our sponsor...
I was recently asked what promoted this donation. It's simple. It started with the biggest truck I'd ever seen in my life unloading more rice than I had ever seen. This at the Skirball?

I made some enquiries and was told that it was Stan's calf. Who is Stan and why is he bringing his calf and rice to the Skirball? Further information led me to Stan's Cafe and *Of All The People*...

It was amazing! Impressive! Emotional! Funny! Frightening! Educational! It was a way of looking at the world and all of us in it using a different tool. It put a different perspective on whole lot of things. It also put a whole lot of things into perspective. I was enthralled but it was there for way too short a time for the public to even know it had come before it had gone. It had to be shared.

What to do? Shockingly, I contacted the Skirball. They didn't call me. I called them. I asked what it would cost to bring the exhibit back for a month. They told me. I fainted. I had never given even 1/10 of that cost to anything or anyone. I gave it deep thought for about thirty seconds, called the bank and wrote the cheque.

Nonny (Anonymous Donor) 19th November, 2007

Under The Radar, World Financial Center, New York
9th - 20th January, 2008

Blog post: We Are Art Souls
The cab driver was Romanian and some kind of slow-burn Gnostic. He learnt we were setting up an art show and

pronounced that there was not enough art in the world. To make art you must have soul and today people are without soul. Having just stepped from the World Financial Centre it wasn't a perspective Amanda, in the front seat, felt moved to contradict. Rocketing up FDR Drive the subject turned to a Future Global Dictatorship, a conspiracy theory he had heard that day and relayed sardonically, as if testing or teasing us.

After slow progress on Monday, the show took shape rapidly on Tuesday and opened yesterday well developed. Ironically the piece looks much better around the highly polished sunlit balcony than in the actual gallery space, which is slightly gloomy with a scruffy concrete floor.

Jack is the poster boy for this incarnation of the show. It's Graeme's picture of him tending rice piles in Bochum that has been picked up by the venue and graces banners and brochures and screens. Five vitrines placed around the public concourses have caused a stir so audience numbers should build from a promising start. The vitrine placed at the entrance to the American Express HQ caused such a stir that some agent of the corporation leapt to phone and check who "authorised"

the use of 65,800 grains of rice to represent their global workforce alongside all the teachers, police officers and taxi drivers in New York City. They also wanted to know where the number had come from. It all got smoothed out easily enough, but such twitchiness makes you want to bundle certain people into a big yellow cab and give them a dose of the slow-burn.

James Yarker 10th January, 2008

Blog post: Making The Most Of It.
[...] Down at the venue things have been going ballistic. The show opened to 50 people, 150 visited on the second [day] and over 300 passed through yesterday. With little media coverage this is a case study of Word of Mouth power. 30,000 people work at the World Financial Centre so we're not going to run out of audience, the question is what will happen over the weekend? [...]

James Yarker 12th January, 2008

The Exchange, Penzance
30th January - 3rd February, 2008

Truro Cathedral
5th - 9th February, 2008

University of Zurich, Schiffbau Schauspielhaus, Zurich
29th February, 2008

Kampnagel Sommer Festival, Hamburg
15th - 23rd August, 2008

Blog Post: Hamburg Get-In - Day 2
[...] Again we have become embroiled in fascinating translation discussions. There often isn't a German equivalent for a word we want to use. Regularly a German word, whilst it means what we want to say, carries an implication of something else, which isn't quite right. Where the English label reads "Tourists Visiting Majorca Last Year", the German translation in effect has to say "Male Tourists and Female Tourists Visiting Majorca Last Year". In reverse English becomes less elegant than German when

writing about "Female Florists in Germany" and "Male Florists in Germany". In German the gender of the florist is communicated with a change of suffix.

James Yarker 13th August, 2008

A.E. Harris Factory, Birmingham
13th September - 5th October, 2008

Blog post: Print - The Next Generation
The last few days have been taken up refining print for the big rice show in Birmingham. We are desperate for this to be a mass appeal event [and have decided that] we need to move onto the fourth generation of publicity material.

The first generation was created before the show was ever performed, Craig's marvellous map of the British Isles made of rice and a grain of rice in the palm of a hand circles with biro and ME written beside it [...]. The second generation came in post-Stuttgart, using Ed [Dimsdale]'s haunting photographs of the rice piles [in that setting]. The third generation responded the demands of venues anxious that photographs [show the] public ideally 'engaging with the show' [...].

Promoting the show ourselves means we have to make the call for Birmingham images. We looked back at the approaches others had taken [and] particularly liked the Norwich and Norfolk Festival's use of a sculptural image on the front with the slogan "Get Things In Perspective", with, on the reverse, the hand – rice grain shot and "Come and Find Yourself" in there somewhere as a strap line. We decided to steal this basic approach.

[We] started to [think] looking at other people looking at rice isn't the way to make the [show] look attractive. We're trying to communicate that this world version is a one-off and yet we're using images of other versions in other places to promote it.
We agreed we needed a new approach, the fourth generation.

We had agreed on a teaser campaign to trail the show. Karen suggested a simple set of images, close ups of individual grains of rice with celebrity names as they might appear in the show. [This] fourth generation harks back to the first generation but with more confidence and clarity. We understand the show now, how it works and why people like it.

I hope everyone's happy with what we've come up with. Late on I picked up a spectacular typo that would have rendered 1/4 of the teaser postcards unusable. If there are any more it's too late, the presses are rolling and soon you can judge for yourselves.

James Yarker 8th August, 2008

Blog post: Global Macro Economics
Global Macro Economics has never felt particularly relevant to me before. I knew eventually it was but now it feels a bit more like being on the frontline.

Now a significant proportion of our income is earned abroad we have become aware of exchange rates coming into play. Whether this has been a period of getting progressively more expensive for people looking to take us to the U.S.A. or us becoming increasingly good value across mainland Europe.
With the prospect of producing a show with 112 tonnes of rice we have suddenly become rather transfixed by commodity prices and the escalating cost of rice.

Now, in the language of BBC financial journalists, 'the credit crunch is starting to bite'. Our 112 tonnes of rice is costing us in the region of £90,000. We buy it in September then sell it back in October and get a healthy portion of that money back, but in the mean time we need to hand over significantly more money that we have at our disposal. This is where you would expect your bank to step in to help.

The HSBC have spent four weeks saying "we can't see there will be a problem with that" and have now said "no". I can't see where the risk is. We buy a commodity which we own and don't intend to destroy. We have a signed contract that it will be bought back. We have cash in the bank to cover the difference in buying and selling prices. We have two more years guaranteed income from Arts Council England, the rice is insured and we have three directors standing personal liability on the loan. How much more security do they want? The threat to "move our account elsewhere" isn't a hollow one and hopefully it will help them see sense.

James Yarker, 16th August, 2008

Blog post: The Big Banner
The factory is still being cleared. The clearers are now being chased around by the cleaners. Furniture has been borrowed from MAC. Today Craig and Arvo picked up Lighting and Sound

kit from store (apparently the *[Cleansing Of] Constance Brown* set has been buried behind *Chitty Chitty Bang Bang*). Jon and I, ably and gamely aided by Poppy, slogged round Birmingham gathering sound kit (16 speakers required). Spirits raised during the slogging around with the sight of this big poster.

If you're based near Birmingham keep your eyes open, there are more.

James Yarker, 27th August, 2008

Blog post: Falling Behind The Rice Race

[...] The rice has been arriving, 26 tonnes per load, one load per day. We've staggered the arrival of this staggering amount of rice so we can deal with it. Normal procedure is to start by building the biggest piles first and then work down to the smallest piles. This time my plan is to focus on small areas and work them up to 'concert pitch' whilst big piles are still being installed elsewhere; the theory being we will then have sections we can show journalists and other visitors that show the piece operating at full strength. We missed our first deadline, Terry Grimley from Birmingham Post visiting at 11am today.

Craig was out and about with Hannah and Robin installing vitrines at key points in town to publicise the show. Graeme has been leading a team building the mountainous pile that will be the [show's] largest statistic. I have been interspersing bouts of fretful plotting with burst of building and production/promotion logistics.

The next deadline and one we can't afford to miss, is having things looking good for a press photo-call timed to coincide with the last lorry's arrival on Thursday.

James Yarker, 3rd September, 2008

Blog post: Storm Warnings

I don't know what it was like where you were, but on Friday night it hammered with rain in Birmingham. It hammered with rain in a way that it seemed meteorologically impossible to sustain for more than ten minutes and it continued like that all night. We'd left 112 tonnes of rice in a factory with 'known leak issues'. Graeme had scored some industrial oil leak absorption fabric sausages which we'd placed in likely looking places, but even so I didn't sleep well on Friday night.

On Saturday I called Collin, Collin called Clive, Clive called in at the venue where Sarah, Eve and I met him. We had a family mopping up and wringing out session. My worst fears were not realised. There were no new leaks and know leaks had not leaked further than feared.

It was however a wise precaution to call in. Water had come within three inches of one particularly vast pile. We revised defensive policies, bowls under drips, fabric sausages lined up protecting the vast pile and containing known seepage. On Monday morning a series of relieved performers related their various damp rice stress dreams.

James Yarker, 8th September, 2008

Blog post: Manual Handling

Today we received our Manual Handling training. It is perhaps now more relevant to the get-out than the get-in, but as the man said "it doesn't have to be a heavy weight to do your back in". He was a personable bloke, who looked like he'd never lifted anything heavier than a box file of risk assessments in his life. He recovered well from finding all the startling or unexpected answers to his early quiz questions were just another specialist subject for finely honed stat minds at the Caff. Percentage injuries at work attributable to manual handling? 38% sounds about right [...]

James Yarker, 8th September, 2008

Blog post: Nearly There
The show is starting to look very much like a show now. There is more to do, but things are well in hand for press photographs and a bit of filming tomorrow. With fire marshal training, new performers arriving, more interviews and opening logistics all intruding I knew I wanted to be well ahead in developing the show and it looks like we're not far off.

A few visitors have been wandering through and giving the appropriate bowled over responses. It is always more impressive than people imagine. Tonight Collin, Paul and I stayed late. The show looks great at night in this space.

The most exciting news for connoisseurs of fine ethical dining, is that The Kitchen Garden Cafe will be running a concession at the show. Most exciting for connoisseurs of the show – we are working on an aesthetic departure. The venue has a side room which has a different feel to the rest of the space and needed a new strategy. This is in place and tentatively being initiated.

One of the things I enjoy most about working on this show is solving the conundrums it throws up. What to do with that room was a new and serious one. It took a bit of conviction and guidance from Craig to commit to a new approach and discard a significant portion of some people's work from yesterday. It will pay off. It gives the show now has an added twist. The secret will be revealed once the show has opened.

James Yarker, 9th September, 2008

Blog post: How Much?
[...] The day wasn't without anxiety. A local news agency, having received a press release, phoned up expressing an interest in the show. Normally this would be a good thing, but their first question was "how much did the show cost?". Now, I don't know about you, but I've never heard a national news story about what excellent value for money a particular work of art is, particularly not one which isn't oil placed on canvas looking a lot like the thing it is 'supposed to be'. So we didn't answer the question and we'll see what happens. Ironically the same agency sent a photographer, who arrived woefully late, but whom we politely accommodated, and he loved the show. He left with a fist full of fliers and a promise to return with his girlfriend. Hopefully this is the start of a crazy word-of-mouth snowball.

James Yarker, 10th September, 2008

Blog post (tweaked): Test Cases
Of All The People In All The World has a few simple rules.
1. Each grain of rice can only represent a PERSON.
2. Each grain of rice can only represent ONE person.
3. That person cannot be fictional.
4. That person can be dead.
5. As the grains act as 'cast members' it is possible for one person to appear in a number of piles simultaneously 'played by' different grains of rice.

There are further rules of protocol, about presentation and performance but it is the boundaries of those first fundamental rules that I enjoy exploring. and here we have to resort to Case Law. Today Chris presented a new Test Case [...]:

Test Case 1: Dugrenier vs (my metaphor breaks down here): The Unknown Soldier.

Dugrenier argued that as a real, though unknown soldier was buried beneath the Arc De Triomphe in the Tomb of the Unknown Soldier she should be allowed to place this person into the show [...]. After some deliberation Justice Yarker denied the claim, his reasoning being that, whilst fulfilling the technical requirements that the rice represent a single, non-fictional person, the symbolic power carried by the real Unknown Soldier collapses when translated into the show as that symbolism is removed by a further degree, it becomes a representation of a symbol. The show makes the role of the Unknown Soldier redundant as every single solider who fell on a particular battle field can now have their own rice representative, they do not have to share a single symbol. In part, this is what gives the show its power. [I'm now no longer so sure about this]

Test Case 2: Rose vs Yarker - Twelve Angry Men
Appealing a previous judicial ruling [Graeme] Rose argued that Twelve Angry Men shouldn't be allowed because amongst other things it 'felt a bit funny'.

Many of the trainee barristers standing by had no idea what was going on and had to be briefed about an old black and white film staring Henry Fonda adapted from a stage play, the author of which no one could remember.

Trow and Semp, speaking on behalf of Yarker, pointed out that whilst the 'statistic' appears to be referring to fictional characters in fact it is merely identifying a dozen hopping mad males. Trow used the Million Men test case to bolster his argument.

Rose internally cursed that QC Hadingue was on other legal duties in Stratford[-Upon-Avon] and unable to back him up.

Yarker (acting contrary to all good legal procedure as both defendant and judge) decided against the appeal. Whilst acknowledging the validity of the 'feeling a bit funny' argument and welcoming the appeal he said he was minded, on this occasion, to allow Twelve Angry Men so long as it stays in the side room and doesn't interfere with any other 'statistics'.

With both case and court dismissed everyone wandered off and no one seemed particularly bothered about being paid less than £100 per hour.

James Yarker, 11th September, 2008

Blog post: Careful Phrasing

[...] Leafing through the two Comments Books after this weekend's opening was a fantastically positive experience, people were gushing with enthusiasm. Yet, nestled amongst the feel good acclamation was one entry that exposes both the limitations and strengths of the comments book.

Someone had taken exception to our use of the term 'Coloured People' in labelling a statistic. The problem with the Comment Book form of feedback is that there's no right of reply. The author was anonymous and long gone. There was no chance of running after them and explaining – "that's not our term! That statistic and those around it are those of apartheid South Africa where 'Coloured' was an official term of the regime. Yes, it is offensive but that's because the regime was offensive".

The advantage of a comments book is that we now know that someone is walking around Birmingham with the belief that Stan's Cafe [are unsound]. Although we'd rather stretch our audience than patronise them on this occasion we felt we could afford to leave things to chance. The whole set of labels now read something like " 'Coloured' People In South Africa 1948 as defined by the Apartheid Regime". It's an ugly label but better than people attaching an ugly phrase to us.

James Yarker 17th September, 2008

Centre de Cultura Contemporania De Barcelona
27th - 30th November, 2008

Festivalul National De Teatru, Bucharest
3rd - 11th November, 2009

Blog post: Taking Over
[...] It turns out that Bucharest, despite presenting some challenges, is a great place to be performing these two shows*. The country's dramatic recent history provides both powerful content and an eager and engaged audience for Of All The People In All The World [...]

James Yarker, 6th November, 2008

*The Cleansing Of Constance Brown was also there.

Wesleyan University, Middletown, Connecticut
21st February - 4th March, 2009

Blog post: Welcome to Middletown
[...] We have been lent a beautiful house here, right beside the Wesleyan University Campus and the others were already looking very at home in the vast kitchen with cats wandering around.

Professor Barry Chernoff*, one of our hosts, came round to escort us to the local bar and introduce us to its beers, which was very considerate of him. Barry is an ichthyologist ("a fish guy") and really great value. It soon became clear 'theatrical anecdotes' weren't going to cut it alongside tales of the Amazon, Piranhas, Sting Rays and fish that at crawl inside your penis if you piss in the water. Perhaps only Werner Herzog could trade stories in this kind of company but who wants to trade when the quality is this high? We fed Barry questions, sat back and had a great time.

James Yarker, 18th February, 2009

*Barry was a huge asset for the show. He set his first year Environmental Science under-graduate students an assignment of generating useful environmental statistics for our show, which were then fact checked by his post-graduate students. The results were fantastic.

Blog post: Haiku
[...] I work on statistics for the vitrines that are poised to be placed around campus. Barry and I talk about Darwin as prep for the Science Department display (later he emails saying there are 27 adult Charles Darwins living in the U.S.). Vitrines are a kind of haiku version of the show, you have to boil it all down to 1m square and keep it elegant in both visually and conceptually. It takes far more time than we ever credit it with.

Eventually Graeme and I nail the Haiku (if you're following the show on Twitter you will already know the poem). We carry everything over to the Science block turning heads as we go. They don't often see a brown housecoat in these parts, still less two together. No doubt a rumour is sweeping campus about this new, quasi-Mormon sect.

All goes well with the vitrine, the rice is tidy, the paper all very neatly, Darwin is there, H.M.S. Beagle is there, local creationists are laid out beside local evolutionists. All is as it should be. We carefully lift the Perspex hood over the display and gently lower it down. Beautiful. We admire our work. All is good, so casually we pull the protective plastic coatings from the Perspex and bundle it up into balls. We're all set to go but inside the vitrine things have gone crazy. Grains for rice are rising up, standing on their ends and leaping from the piles. They're pinging themselves against the Perspex attempting to escape and the paper is curling at its edges attempting to catch them. Momentarily our allegiances in the Creation – Evolution debate swing decisively [religious], then the crackle of static electricity breaks out. Now we're spinning and dancing with delight. It's fantastic, now this extraordinary show even has its own weird, flea-show style variety act, should a cabaret opening come up [...]

The Harbourfront Centre, Toronto
13th - 24th May, 2009

Mayfest, The Island, Bridewell, Bristol
14th - 16th May, 2009

Greenbelt Festival, Cheltenham
28th - 31st August, 2009

Aberystwyth Arts Centre
30th September - 3rd October, 2009

Domaine d'O, Montpellier, France
21st September - 2nd October, 2009

India Forum, Reitschule, Bern
14th - 30th January, 2010

We were brought to Bern by the CESCI (The Centre for Socio-Cultural Interaction) which is based in Tamil Nadu in India with a support association in Switzerland as part of their India Forum. Alongside us there were talks, films and performances looking at themes of hunger, land rights and non violent protest.

We were based in the great hall of The Reitschule once, as the name suggests, a riding school, but now a vibrant, left leaning cultural and community centre which hosts bands, theatre, films and exhibitions. The hall provided a very atmospheric setting for the show but a cold one, so cold that it made @AE Harris seem positively barmy, so cold that even the printer refused to work. To get over this we had to reside for much of the time in a small office/cupboard which could be heated, print out sheets and then scurry out into the cold place to lay out new piles. Once the show opened we were furnished with a pub style patio heater and warm sweet cups of chai tea.

The context of the show (India, Switzerland and the UK) threw up some interesting research and juxtapositions of statistics. For example, the same number of people were born in Switzerland last year as are born in India each day and both countries have the same number of daily McDonalds customers.

Salisbury International Arts Festival, Salisbury Cathedral
27th - 31st May, 2010

A sermon preached in the Cathedral:
"To see a world in a grain of sand" wrote William Blake in his Auguries of Innocence:

"To see a world in a grain of sand,
And a heaven in a wild flower,
Hold infinity in the palm of your hand
And eternity in an hour."

But for the fact that one cannot improve on the genius of William Blake, I was tempted this morning to rewrite his verse to read something like...

"To see our world in a mound of rice"

...confronted as we have been this weekend with the amazing spectacle (produced here for us by Stan's Cafe as part of this year's Salisbury Festival) of mounds of rice, large and small, which have got under the skin of our world and under the skin

of our imagination. I met Maria Bota, the festival director, in town yesterday and she and I enthused together about the 'rice show' and she said: "You know that rice gets everywhere: don't tell anyone but it does". Well I am telling you because that rice does get everywhere, and most of all it gets into our imagination. For these mounds of rice stop us in our tracks and make us think afresh with curiosity, amazement, amusement (as we contemplate the idea of thirteen people crammed into a

Smart car!) or with solidarity as we sympathise with the one person who left their glasses behind in the Cathedral last year, who could so easily have been one of us. But most of all, we see our world made not out of continental land masses divided by oceans but out of islands of rice, which are more revealing than any statistics or economic forecasts. And they are more revealing perhaps because these mounds of rice bring the anonymous and distant world home to us, right here where we are. And we, of course, although standing and looking and wondering or laughing, are grains of rice. We may not be Nick Clegg or David Cameron but we are grains of rice in the UK's population, illustrated by the mound of rice here at the spire crossing. We have been part of the mound who make up McDonalds customers and we are amongst those who were stranded abroad during the volcano induced flight ban.

In one respect this fascinating exhibition has been arranged with no comment – simply an accurate as can be factual label to accompany each mound. But these rice mounds have not been arranged randomly. There may be no analysis or moral judgement: but the juxtapositions of, for example, the numbers of refugees in the world next to the almost equal number of millionaires in the world, and the fluctuating number of children who died from curable diseases in 1988, 2001 and 2008 invite us to make our own judgement and come to our own conclusions. As Blake suggested, we can see a world in a grain of sand.

Those of us who came to the Monteverdi Vespers last Wednesday in the Cathedral may ask what this exhibition of rice mounds has to do with art. But art, surely, emerges from a creative idea, that reveals our world in new and sometimes shocking or startling ways and kindles our imagination and transforms our perceptions, so that somehow in our moral or spiritual being we are changed. If that is the meaning and purpose of art, then this exhibition Of All the People in All the World must be in the same boat of human endeavour as the Monteverdi Vespers.

Having mounds of rice in the Cathedral today provides a wonderful diversion for any preacher. Because today is Trinity Sunday, when we are confronted with the ineffable mystery, which brings us to the heart of our Christian faith, and which preacher after preacher has tried to explain but which, because the doctrine of the Trinity is both ineffable and a mystery, cannot be explained.

It cannot be explained – even though at every service here, as we shall do shortly, we affirm our belief in the Trinitarian God who reveals himself as Father, Son and Holy Spirit; it cannot be explained but it can be grasped, or more accurately we can be grasped by it. Like so much doctrine which cannot merely be learned and assented to, the reality of the Trinity is like a penny dropping in our imagination and our consciousness. We may describe the Holy Trinity as best we may in doctrinal formulations but our words are useless in grasping its profound simplicity. Perhaps the penny drops most of all when at some point of grief or pain or shame or transforming love or happiness or achievement that humbles us, we are reduced to silence – or rather raised to silence – and in our contemplation of the God who is love, we know that we are loved. Then the Trinity grasps us and becomes a reality not a doctrine.

Having said what I truly believe about Christian doctrine, that it is not something to be learned and assented to, or recited in a formulaic way, it is something to be experienced, lived out, discovered and recognised as true, as the words of Christian belief dissolve into the silence of Christian belonging. Having said that, I should be true to my word and shut up and sit down.

But I can't quite resist the temptation to make some connection between Stan's Cafe's exhibition and this Feast of the Holy Trinity. Perhaps God is Stan: and Stan, though having one name, is in fact three people who work hard together to make a living from offering hospitality to anyone who comes through the door. The only qualification for entry to Stan's Cafe is that they are hungry: hungry for bread and hungry for companionship – which after all simply means others to break bread with.

Stan, Stan and Stan, who run the café, provide just that: a warm welcome, bread on the table, a glass of wine, and their companionship. The hungry traveller is refreshed and feels he or she could stay longer. He is told he can stay forever: this is his home if he wants it. And then, as he finishes his food and wipes his mouth on his sleeve, the traveller sees there are others sitting at other tables, and others coming in at the door. They are all different – all completely different – which makes our traveller by turns suspicious, frightened, jealous, resentful: perhaps this "home" which seemed so idyllic isn't so congenial after all. But the three Stans introduce our traveller to other travellers and get some newcomers to sit at his table. They get them talking together by telling them the story of their own lives: The Life of Stan they call it. It's an amazing story - of passion and love, of friendships made and broken, of unspeakable cruelty and tear-jerking heroism, of wrongs forgiven and lives re-made. At one point, the three Stans show the marks of some terrible injustice on their hands and feet: and yet through it all they have stayed together and afterwards decided to make their home a home for all – a home for all the people in all the world, you might say.

The Stans' storytelling at first reduced everyone to silence: it was so moving: suddenly everyone felt they were really in the same place, not just physically but emotionally. And then the Stans said: "Now it's your turn: you all have stories: tell them. We will give you each a mound of rice, take one grain and put it on your plate – that's you, each one of you a single grain of rice, and as you tell your stories, add a grain of rice every time you mention someone who is part of your story. And so they did. All night long, in small groups and large, they told their stories to each other and made their mounds of rice out of the people they had met as the story of the world unfolded.

As dawn broke, they were talked out. There were hundreds if not thousands of mounds of rice representing the whole of humanity. No one was fearful or suspicious or resentful any more, as they had heard such wonderful stories about how to be human. Tired though they were, they were ready to eat: "Come and have breakfast" said Stan. And the three Stans took the mounds of rice from each of the travellers and put the rice into a vast cauldron full of spices and herbs. The rice when it was cooked was able to feed them all deliciously, but they had learned from their storytelling that those who were nearest to the cauldron of food needed to provide first of all for those who were furthest away at the back of the queue.

"The first shall be last and the last shall be first":

Stan quipped, and he winked at the two other Stans.
Canon Jeremy Davies, Trinity Sunday 30th May, 2010

Oldham Festival Of Diversity, Gallery Oldham
7th - 28th September, 2010

Setagaya Public Theatre, Tokyo
14th - 22nd September, 2010

Tokyo OATP Get In Day 1
Everything progresses smoothly and there are some deft Japanese touches. Our computers are all linked without wires to the printer (cue Chimpanzee with furrowed brow prodding printer with index finger). The table cloth is the brightest greenest and best ever. The rice is the bulkiest ever so we're down to 52 grains per gram and have had to send out for more supplies. The local brushes are beautiful and Jon's box of tricks has done the trick and we have tannoy announcements. We don't even have to learn Japanese as local theatre maker and polymath Kakumoto Atsushi is here helping us out.
James Yarker, 13th September, 2010

Blog post: Opening In Setagaya
[...] For non-rice obsessives all you need know is that the show opened in good shape, [d]evotees only need read on.
Information no one really needs to know: Representing an F1 Pit Stop in rice is best done with Long Grain not what we have here. Japanese Emperors can change their name whenever

they fancy – which makes writing a label for them more controversial than you would imagine. The Japanese ministry for transport will phone you back to tell you how many driving instructors and examiners there are in the country if you phone up and ask nicely. Reading about ritual suicide in ancient Japan will turn your stomach. The Japanese language, both written and spoken appears to get more not less difficult the more you learn about it. The process of translation is fascinating.

Finally; Nihonjin's *Too Many People* is a very bad track to play at a private view – even if they are/were locals and Spiro works out much better.

James Yarker 15th September, 2010

Hall Of Nations, Kennedy Center, Washington DC
1 - 7 November 2010

Blog post: Washington Despatch
The Stan team took some time out from the first day of the get-in here in Washington to show our faces at the British Ambassador's official residence, a swanky reception was held for visiting artists and the great and the good from the Kennedy Center and British council. A be-kilted piper played as we were let in through the gates and although there was a disappointing absence of Ferrero Rocher the Ambassador did spoil us with delicious butler-served canapés and aperitifs. With the speeches over we raced back to the venue to finish the get-in and were stopped in our tracks by how the work we had already done looked. Now that it was dark outside the lighting installed by the Kennedy Center technicians added an extraordinary glow to the rice which was reflected in the polished marble walls and floors of the Hall of Nations and was complimented, both aesthetically and thematically, by the permanently lit flags of the world that adorn the length of the space. Even if we say so ourselves it was beautiful.

– some time later –

We're now entering the final 48 hours of our stay and the show is being well received. It's seems that it is not what the regular Kennedy crowd is used to but we're attracting quite a buzz. The crowd swells substantially between 6pm and 8pm when we get the folks that happen upon the show on their way to see other things in the eight or so formal and informal spaces around the centre.

Washington, being the political centre of the 'free world', is highly sensitised, some punters are finding it hard not to be suspicious about whether we're trying to push a political agenda through the show. It's not surprising though when you consider, one way or another, around 300,000 people in this city (over half its population) work in the government and that the word 'Lobbyist' has etymological claims to being coined here by President Ulysses S. Grant when he would be pestered by activists while he was trying to enjoy his nightly drink and cigar in the lobby of the Willard Hotel. Some people are more satisfied than others by our assurances that our primary motivation is to simply tell stories – stories of no intentional political partiality. Either way the conversations we have had have thoroughly and engagingly explored the very nature of statistics and the standards and scrutiny we who make the show, as well as those who see the show, apply to the statistical information we all consume every day.

Jack Trow, 7th November, 2010

India Forum, Reitschule, Bern
15th - 31st January, 2011

No Strings Attached Festival, Mainz
13th - 16th May, 2011

Palais de Glace, Buenos Aires
8th - 17th July, 2011

Blog post: Prep & Prep
[...] Craig and I have been getting stuck into research for OATP [in Buenos Aries]. We have some historic statistics already translated into Spanish from earlier gigs in Spain but this is our first trip with the show to South America. Working in a new culture with a such a politically charged recent history makes it an exciting challenge. There is a lot of local suspicion of the National Statistics Office and loads of stuff is in a language we don't speak, it is properly challenging but I love doing this research, I could happily spend weeks doing it.

James Yarker 30th June, 2011

Blog post: Penultimate Day in B.A.
Today is the penultimate day of *Of All The People In All The World* in Buenos Aires, I won't bother posting any more images as you can find an exhaustive inventory of this performance via visitors to its Facebook Page. This page is worth both a look and a 'like' as each 'like' means the sponsors, Gallo Arroz, donate a portion of rice to [our hosts] Banco de Alimentos [food bank]. We're up to about 2,500 portions now, which as the food bank feed 78,000 people per day doesn't sound too impressive, until you factor in the 5,000kg they have already donated via the show. Get with the 'liking' [...]

James Yarker, 16th July, 2011

Interrogate Festival, Dartington
23rd - 24th September, 2011

WOMAD Earthstation Festival, Adelaide
21st - 23rd October, 2011

Blog post: Memphis Rice
News in of the largest scale emulation of Of All The People In All The World. St. Francis of Assisi Catholic School in Cordova. Having seen the show in Washington D.C. they took on their own version. For those who know the show seeing these photos will be a bit eerie, don't say you haven't been warned. Stan's Cafe gets a good acknowledgement within their story.
James Yarker, 5th March, 2012

Paccar Room, The RSC, Stratford Upon Avon
14th April - 31st July, 2012

Blog post: RSC - OATP
Our first day here with the show open has been great with lots of interested visitors and positive comments. We are here for three months but intend to keep the show moving and dynamic throughout. Whilst using many statistics that we include in other versions of the show we are also here responding to themes addressed in productions running during the RSC season and to the times in which Shakespeare lived. This has thrown up interesting combinations, including a run of statistics looking at the growth of the slave trade from the Elizabethan era, via Francis Drake through to Martin Luther King speaking in Washington.
Craig Stephens, 14th April, 2012

Blog post: Last Chance to See
After an extraordinarily long and successful run at the R.S.C. in Stratford-Upon-Avon Of All The People In All The World is packed up tomorrow evening.

The low-light was the piece being vandalised early on during a private function. The highlight was all the brilliant audience feedback. The most curious moment was Prince Charles visiting the piece with none of us being allowed in whilst he was there – a view so private the performers aren't even allowed to be there – fortunately the same was not true of Julius Caesar.

Craig Stephens, 31st July, 2012

Perth International Arts Festival
6th February - 2nd March 2013

Blog post: 'Bump In' Day 3
One of the many peculiarities about *Of All The People In All The World* is that it can easily feel as if you are making a show that must be ready for the Opening Night. This is because you come without a script or a stage plan and have to make it all up. I find myself growing anxious that we won't be 'finished' in time, however this is the wrong way to think about the situation. We are doing a 'Bump In', the race is to be ready to start not finish the show. The problems that have to be solved are: what cues do we want to start improvising from and where should the props (rice) go? The challenge is to open in a state that is already a satisfying balanced piece but has space enough to develop for three weeks[...]

James Yarker 8th February, 2013

Two Snow Hill, Birmingham
12th - 21st April, 2013

When Dawn at Headline Communications approached us saying that her clients Hines and Ballymore were interested in commissioning a large version of the show to mark the opening of a very large shiny new office block they were building in central Birmingham our ears pricked up. It had been nearly five years since the show was last in its home city and ten years since its first performance. Our experience from Newcastle was that newly completed offices are beautiful settings for the show and at Two Snowhill we would be on the sixth floor with ceiling to floor windows and spectacular views over North Birmingham. "Are we interested? Yes, very".

CAST AND CREW OF THE FILM "VERTIGO"

Each new version of the show needs structure and here we drew inspiration from the view, the real world beyond the class. Hence a view of the BT Tower inspires statistics about mobile phone use, Snow Hill Station leads to statistics about travel and commuting, the Jewellery Quarter provokes us to think of industry, the Salvation Army buildings cause us to reflect on homelessness and St. Chads obviously introduces the new Pope and religion.

The show caused a lot of positive comments from the developers and their guests at the private view. Pieces in the local press, radio, TV and on-line coverage resulted in audiences queuing at the doors to get in on the first two days.

St Martin's Church Parish Centre, Worcester
28th July - 1st August, 2014

**The Great Charter Festival,
Royal Holloway University, Egham**
14th June, 2015

We were invited to be part of the Great Charter Festival - 'a one day summer fair with a radical twist' which commemorated the 800th anniversary of the sealing of the Magna Carta. Our venue was the rather splendid setting of the Dining Hall in the Founders Building at Royal Holloway University. The university is sited just a few miles from the field in Runnymede where the charter was sealed and this one day festival incorporated lots of activities celebrating its legacy.

This proved to be an interesting context for the show - the Magna Carta has had an influence around the world on the concept of the rule of law, personal freedom and the power of governments. This gave us the opportunity to explore statistics around the legal system, the history of protest, our changing relationship with the royal family and the fight for suffrage [...]

Theater Bonn: Save The World II, Halle Beuel, Bonn
18th - 20th September, 2015

While one team had fun placing *Of All The People In All The World* in a big carpentry workshop, next door James was devising a brief performance called *Small People With Big Feet* with scientists.

Theater Freiburg @ Meckelhalle, Sparkasse Bank, Freiburg
12th - 20th February, 2016

Having staged the show in Bonn in September the rice remained in Germany and made the journey south to be reused here in Freiburg [...] *Of All The People In All The World* was programmed as part of the theatre's 'Face The Face' season which included a range of work looking at how stories, memories and history are shared and how an audience interacts with the artistic presentation of these. [...] On the final day, as part of a cultural heritage project collaboration between Theater Freiburg and The Museum of Modern Art, audience members were invited to take away small prepared bags of rice. They signed their names in a museum record book and in so doing became rice custodians for a year, promising to return their grains in March 2017.

During the year they will consider who the grains of rice in their care might represent - to think about what are significant personal, national or international moments and record their ideas. In twelve months time we will all gather again in the museum to re-stage the show, using the rice that has been returned and some of the statistics that the rice custodians have recorded. Their grains of rice will be re-cast in a show that will look at what might have changed over the year for the individual, for Freiburg, for the world. We are looking forward to returning and making new discoveries.

Craig Stephens

Blog post: How To Do It

I live in fear of Tim Harford. He hosts the Radio 4 and BBC World Service program *More Or Less*. The premise of this brilliant programme is that they interrogate statistics that have entered the public realm but sound a bit dubious. Classically it is politicians who are subject to fact checking but the programme's range is broad, it's up-beat and playful; Tim Harford is fantastic but he terrifies me.

My interest in statistics will be well known to any regular follower of Stan's Cafe. Our performance installation *Of All The People In All The World* is entirely built on statistics, it is our biggest hit and virtually everyone loves it. When we first performed the show my greatest fear was that visitors would spend all their time questioning the integrity of all the statistics in the show. It was difficult to work our what counted as 'due diligence' for statistics we included in this artwork but we did our best.

In the event I was surprised to find very few people questioned the numbers and when they did these were usually numbers we had questioned ourselves and done extra work on verifying. Yet ultimately, it is an work of art not a government report, so although we would divide the 73.4 Million people who traveled through Heathrow Airport last year by 365 to reduce the amount of double counting and label this "People who travel through Heathrow Airport each day" (aesthetically I'd rather say

"Yesterday" than "Each Day" but this would imply an unjustifiable level of precision). Of course my fear is that Tim Harford will land on the show and point out that this new number fails to account for passengers who use Heathrow for connecting flights and are thus counted twice in the day, once as an Arrival and again as a Departure, or for business passengers who fly to a destination and return on the same day. The man could make mince meat of the show! Except he always comes across as a very reasonable chap, so I'm sure he'd understand.

Anyway, my admiration for Tim Harford was increased today when I heard his recent TED Talk which starts with the amazing story behind Keith Jarrett's Köln Concert, which I'd never heard before and then went on to make an argument for 'mess' and 'disruption' being a valuable element of a creative process.

James Yarker, 21st January, 2016

The Library of Birmingham
15th - 19th April, 2016

Great Fire 350, Inner Temple, City of London
30th August - 4th September, 2017

We were holding off presenting the show in London until the correct opportunity came along. An invitation to be part of a program of arts events commemorating the 350 anniversary of The Great Fire of London felt like just the kind of opportunity we were holding out for. The gig grew even more attractive when producers Artichoke secured the City of London's Inner Temple Hall as a venue.

The performance used two tonnes of rice and was themed around fire and its consequences. We had nearly 3,500 visitors and occasionally had to use a queuing system to make sure everyone had space to enjoy the show.

The show's highlight was a proposal of marriage (and its

acceptance) within the show. Performer Gareth Nicholls found his name in the show and his partner proposing, they added their grains of rice to a sheet of paper to mark the event and this statistic became the basis of a section about civil partnerships and gay marriage.

A twin statistic was added to the show being performed simultaneously in Basel.

Theaterfestival Basel
30th August - 5th September, 2016

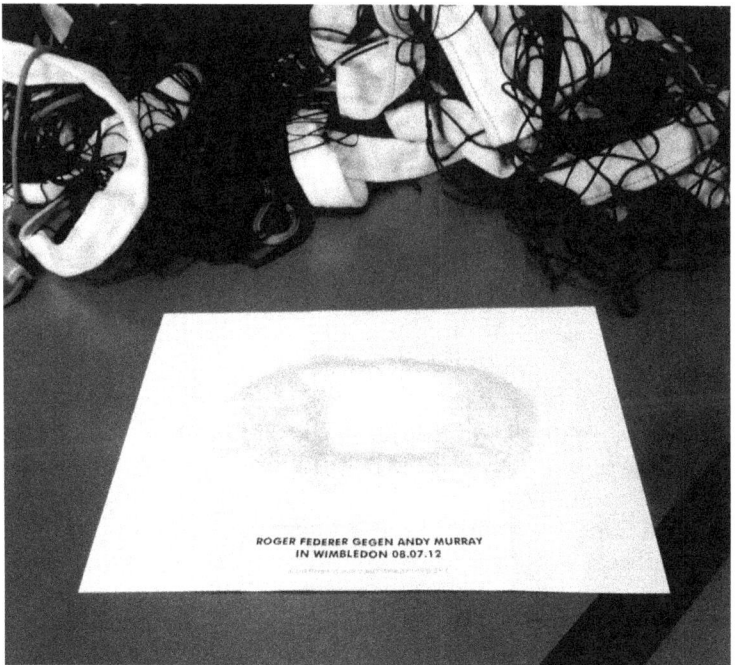

Blog Rice Etiquette
[...] Usually my role during the get-in is close to the table shaping the show and because I am usually returning home after the opening and missing the performance, I tend not to have a great deal to do with the local performers. On this

occasion Craig was at the table and I found myself starting to do bits of induction for the new performers, as well as being fun this also reminded me of the subtle code of etiquette involved in performing the show. This preferred way of doing things has built up over time and although some of it is collated in a performer's handbook, much like an apprenticeship it is best learned whilst performing.

Early on the opening night a small child stood on a sheet of A4 paper, which had a small pile of rice on it. The dampness of their bare foot caused the sheet to adhere and as they moved their foot so the rice went flying. Mortified the child's father tried to make good, but that's not his job, a performer had to step in and remember a few key points.

Sweep every grain up, if you are not confident you have all the rice it should be re-counted or re-weighed. Never walk with rice balanced on a sheet of paper, always transfer it to a bowl. If paper is damaged it must be replaced. Never leave a labelled sheet of paper on the floor without its statistic on it. Ideally if replacing a sheet the rice for that sheet should be left in place in a bowl, this looks good so don't rush to replace the sheet of paper.

It is difficult to make the switch from 'get-in mode' to 'performance mode'. In the get-in you are trying to do as much as possible as quickly as possible to the highest possible level. In performance mode you need to ease off. As Craig pointed out standing or walking around with a warm but slightly proprietorial air is often a good use of your time [...]

James Yarker, 1st September, 2016

Homo Novis Festival, Riga
8th - 11th November, 2016

Blog post: Par ikvienu cilvēku visā pasaulē
Every five years or so I like to put up a post about translation, that time has come around again and this is the post.

This week a festival in Latvia asked us:
"Dear Roisin, we have to translate the title of the work into Latvian and I wanted to ask you to explain in what way you use "of all the people…" to have exact translation"

What a beautiful question. I love all this stuff about the use of words. So if you don't want to know the 'official answer' then stop reading right now.

Principally "of" in this context means "about" so it is a show "About all the people in all the world" as in "the story of all the people in all the world". The superfluous second "all" in the title is intended to evoke that famous line in the film Casablanca, "Of all the gin joints in all the towns in all the world she walks into mine" (about 95 minutes in) which hopefully implies "of all the people in all the world it had to be you".

The show is about EVERYONE and ONE PERSON at the same time, in my mind at least the slight ambiguity of the title allows both readings to coexist. Of course it may not work in Latvian. I'm not even sure it works in English!

Roisin [Caffrey, (Executive Producer)] came up with a simpler, more elegant formulation:
"Of all the people in all the world, these… were born today."
"Of all the people in all the world, these… are firefighters in Riga."

Which should probably become the new 'official answer'.
James Yarker, 7th October, 2016

Compass Festival, Central Library, Leeds
16th - 19th November, 2016

Theater Freiburg & Museum für Neue Kunst, Freiburg
4th - 9th April, 2017

As the 2016 performance in Freiburg drew to a close, members of the public were asked to take away and look after a bag of rice for a year. A museum archive book was completed detailing what 'art work' was out on loan to which person. During the year that followed these custodians were asked to photograph their rice in their home and to perhaps record population statistics that interested them through the year.

In 2017, in a small room in the Museum für Neue Kunst with the remains of another installation stored beside us we built a small version of our show displaying statistics linked to but updated from last year's, including statistics covering significant events that had happened in the intervening time.

On the walls we installed the photographs of the rice in storage and as these bags were returned they were placed underneath the photographs. We started to create new areas of the show responding to the ideas and numbers brought back by the custodians.

The most significant new element for this presentation and the element that gave it the alternative title *The Great Art Giveaway* was a focused on sealing rice in labelled bags and giving it away. The labels explained that the bag was an art object, but that if the owner wished to eat the rice then this was possible so long as it was washed and well cooked. Over the first four days more than 400 bags were made of varying sizes. These were given away to visitors to the exhibition. On the fifth and sixth days a table was set up in the street outside the gallery and rice bags given away from there.

On the final day all the statistics laid out in the show were sealed in bags with archive labels identifying them. These were left with the gallery as the installation in kit form ready for storage.

Rice not stored in the museum and not taken by the public was donated to a local zoo.

Impulse Theater Festival, Ringlokschuppen Ruhr, Mulheim
26th - 29th June, 2017

For this presentation we collaborated with the Ruhr branch of The Silent University. This organisation brings together refugees, asylum seekers and migrants with professional or academic backgrounds in their countries of origin who can no longer use their expertise in their current situations. It provides a platform for participants to share knowledge and skills and highlights the breadth of experience held within the migrant community.

Blog post: New brush

Real live post with a hand written address is always exciting and when the envelope is colourful, cushioned and from Sri Lanka its arrival is a major event. I couldn't imagine what could be inside or why it may be addressed to me. Then, as the thin bristled hand brush dropped out I recalled a conversation I'd had a few weeks ago in Mulheim and it all made sense.

Of All The People In All The World was in Mulheim and I'd just spoken at the official opening when a woman came up to me and started asking me about the brushes we used. It was an unusual start to a conversation because although we choose the brushes carefully we don't consider them a particularly noteworthy element of a show that provokes so much debate in other directions. Nevertheless the woman was interested in the brushes so we talked brushes. It emerged that she had recently been bequeathed a collection of brushes on the death of a friend. She evidently wasn't keen on continuing the collection but at the same time sentiment prevented her disposing of the collection unthinkingly – she wondered if we could make use of one of the brushes which was similar in design to those we already used. I replied that that we would be honoured to adopt this brush, that it would be put to good use and the story of its journey to us would be added to the richness of all subsequent shows.

So now you've heard it, the story of the new brush.
James Yarker, 17th August, 2017

Sommerszene 2018, Salzburg
8 - 16 June, 2018

Blog post: Of all the people in Salzburg
We have just returned from spending ten days at the Sommerszene 2018 Festival in Salzburg where we performed Of All The People In All The World in the beautiful setting of the Kollegienkirche.
Around 7,000 people saw the show during our time there, people from all over the world. Below are some observations on some members of the audience, collected over one hour on the final afternoon (16th June 2018) …
People looking down at piles of amber rice.
People looking up at white Baroque domes.
A boy with a pirate T-shirt and a girl with a top that says Love.
A couple with rucksacks, a guitar and a neatly rolled tent.
A woman with a crutch, a couple holding hands.
Three women with heart shaped biscuit necklaces with the initials S and F spelled out in icing.
A pregnant woman with her hand on her back.
A man with shoes but no socks.

Green plimsolls, white plimsolls, blue plimsolls. Green suede shoes, brown leather shoes, trainers with stripes and trainers with ticks. Sandals, sandals, sandals, walking shoes, espadrilles, high heels, sandals and socks, painted toe nails.
A tour guide describes in German.
A man drips ice cream.
A woman coughs, a man sneezes, a family laughs.
Two girls giggle on a bench.
A man takes his girlfriends's hand.
Arms folded, hands tucked into trouser waistband, hands

behind backs, a hand on a chin, hands in pockets, hands pointing.
A woman puts coins into the box on the votive stand and lights a candle.
A man dips his hand into holy water, crosses himself and backs out of the church.
A mother strokes the head of her baby held in a sling.
A woman kneels and says a prayer.
A baby cries in a pushchair.
Several pink shirts, a jumper draped over shoulders, stripy shirts and spotty shirts, a traditional Austrian dress, denim shorts, lederhosen, jeans with rips in the knees.
A girl runs around dodging piles of rice.
A father lifts up his daughter with one arm.
A man pushes his wife in a wheelchair.
A woman nods in agreement to her friend.
A father strokes his daughter's arm.
Straw hats, baseball caps, bicycle helmets, dreadlocks, green hair, pink hair, no hair. Two full beards, close cropped stubble, a beard on a chin, a moustache that twirls at the ends.
A woman walks tentatively with two alpine walking sticks.
A girl takes a rest in her little sister's pushchair.
People write messages on their mobile phones.
A man in a red checked shirt has a heated debate with a man in a linen jacket.
People take photographs of rice and architecture and each other.
A red leather handbag, shopping bags from expensive looking shops, cakes in a clear plastic bag, a pretzel in a paper bag.
Sunglasses worn on the face, on the tops of heads, on a chain around the neck, clipped onto shirts by one of the arms.
People from Austria, Italy, the USA, India, France, Scotland, England, Brazil, Japan…
People who look like people you know.

Craig Stephens, 19th June, 2018

Conde Duque, Madrid
12th - 29th September, 2018

Grow Festival, Corby
25th - 27th July, 2019

DreamBIG Festival, Drill Hall, Adelaide
22nd - 31st May, 2019

Blog post: Dream Big Adelaide
[...] Here in Adelaide we have been invited to be part of Dream Big Children's Festival and we are excited because, although children have always enjoyed this show and we have made versions of the show with children, we have never made the show for children before.

I think children like the show because it is tangible and easily comprehensible; it is also a landscape ripe for exploration, discovery and open to sharing, questioning and discussion; you don't have to sit down, you don't have to shut up, there is no 'end' that you have to stay until – pretty much the only thing you mustn't do is step on the rice.

Thus far constructing a "children's version" appears to be a doddle.

Having said that children like the show there are also many, many ways in which the show is inaccessible to children, it uses arch cultural references they've never heard of, to make tangental allusions to dilemmas adults struggle to untangle. While we put a lot of work into the show we leave an enormous amount of work for the audience to do and a lot of that work based on a knowledge of history and politics, an appreciation of irony and bathos and learning a kind of kit form surrealism. If you take all that out because the children won't get it then what do you have left? Is it still *Of All The People In All The World*?

I've come to the conclusion that I'm sure you've already reached. No, with all that removed the show wouldn't be the show any more, but that doesn't matter because there's no way we're taking any of that out just because the children won't understand it! For heaven sake, lots of the adults don't understand it either and that's not us being all superior, while we're making the show we have to explain much of it it to each other. If everyone understood everything all the time it would all be an entirely pointless undertaking.

So for Dream Big we are making a version in which nothing is cut out, but in which the balance is different. For adults we probably wouldn't bother weighing out the populations of the country's seven biggest cities and arranging them around the hall in an approximation of their geography. For adults, to our shame, we probably wouldn't have researched the greatest number of people playing Fortnite simultaneously. There are more statistics about children than in previous versions and fewer references that couldn't be explained to a child in less than a minute. There will still be many opportunities for people to ask a question that leads to a story and a conversation and that is what the show is about.

Making it been fun so far – but then the doors have yet to open to 100 five year olds freshly unleashed from a school bus.

James Yarker, 21st May, 2019

European Forum Alpbach
17th - 30th July, 2019

Blog post: Heavy Activist Rice
When staging *Of All The People In All The World* on foreign shores we always have at least a ton of rice on our rider. It's not very rock-and-roll but when you're building an installation that converts human population statistics into grains of rice it is necessary.

In truth we are starting to sound ever more like theatre's answer to Celine Dion as we get ever more particular about the exact kind of rice we require. We use a grains-per-gram equation to help us 'count' large numbers and so, a few years ago, had to throw an hysterical strop when a venue supplied us with broken rice. Rice with a high proportion of broken grains is significantly cheaper than standard rice but we rely on a high proportion of whole grains to be confident in our counting strategy.

Here in Alpbach, although the rice is our standard long grain white variety it is par-boiled, which has two consequences.

Firstly the rice is approximately 20% heavier per grain than we are used to (presumably it absorbs some water in the par-boiling process). This means we've had to adjust our grain-per-gram equation, keep mindful of the fact that we have fewer grains to play with than we were expecting and that the rice we do use will take up more space than it normally does. A population that we would usually expect to squeeze onto an A4 sheet may now require an A3 sheet.

Secondly, a more subtle result of par-boiling is that when poured the rice piles sit less steeply on the paper and loose grains are more 'lively' than usual, spreading across the paper more widely and readily. It maybe that the par-boiling washes the grains, making them less powdery and thus more slippery than when raw. Whatever the reason the solution is careful sculpting of piles and scrupulous sweeping.

Neither issue is an active problem but this experience will lead us to refine our rice rider [...]

James Yarker, 18th August, 2019

Chipping Norton Arts Festival
5th October 2019

Attenborough Centre for the Creative Arts, Brighton
25th - 27th November, 2019

2019 marked the 50th anniversary of the Basil Spence designed [arts centre]. To mark this our show included a number of statistics related to the year 1969, such as the number of people born in that year in the UK (which scarily includes a couple of us). It was interesting to look back on that year's events which included Vietnam war peace marches, student protests and the beginning of 'The Troubles' in Northern Ireland.
Craig Stephens

The Mail Centre Takeover Nine Elms, Wandsworth
15th - 26th January, 2020

Of All The Creatures Across The Globe

IFTR World Congress, University of Warwick
28ᵗʰ July - 1ˢᵗ August, 2014
Revived
10ᵗʰ - 24ᵗʰ July, 2015

Blog post: Diamond Scales
The notion of doing an animal version of *Of All The People In All The World* had been an intriguing idea floating around for a few years. A few months ago Professor Baz Kershaw approached us with an opportunity to deploy the idea. He planned to create three 'Meadow Meanders' for a big international theatre conference at Warwick University and invited us to contribute animal statistics to his walks. The opportunity seemed too fun to turn down.

The premise is identical to *Of All The People In All The World* one of something represents one of something else. 1 grain of white rice still = 1 human but now 1 pepper corn = 1 mountain gorilla and 1 red lentil = 1 locust etc.

In 2003 trying to establish the average weight of a grain of rice armed only with a set of kitchen scales and a bag or rice was a pain and not a pain I was prepared to go through with 20 different food stuffs. Now, however, we are based in the Jewellery Quarter borrowing a set of diamond scales is as easy as knocking on your neighbour's door. Our neighbours were embarrassed that their most precise scales were unavailable but with those 10 times less accurate our man Phil 'Precision' Holyman was able to compare the weights of individual brown mustard seeds (Wildebeests). His greatest revelation was that 100s and 1000s (one for each known species in the world's oceans) may be so called because of the great variation in their weights (for those thinking the obvious question – no, there appears to be no correlation between colour and weight of the 100 or 1000). [...]

James Yarker, 23rd July, 2014

Blog post: Animal Set Up
Whilst Craig and Jack researched human statistics for *Of All The People In All The World* in St. Martin's Church, Worcester, which opens on Monday, I saw to various jobs around the office and beyond before zipping over to the University of Warwick to complete the installation of statistics for Of *All The Creatures Across The Globe*. After eleven years dealing exclusively with white rice it is a great joy to be parlaying with pepper corns and pumpkin seeds, black sesame and almonds, chick peas and mung beans, red lentils and sago.

It was Shady Brady weather but a supply of cool water kept coming and a gang of assistants helped speed things along. The boxes are looking good in the meanders and responses from bystanders seemed very strong, so hopefully a lot of people will get to enjoy the piece and hopefully we will get some more life from what has been a logistics heavy project.

James Yarker, 24th July, 2014

Everyone Born In The United Kingdom: 1947

1947 was the year in which more children were born in the United Kingdom than any other year, one of them was David Bowie. Having seen our show at the RSC Geoffrey Marsh, Director of Theatre and Performance at the V&A wanted to commission one of our rice piles for the *Bowie Is* exhibition he was curating. We persuaded him that a light box would work better and he agreed.

Blog post: Fame!
If you get to see the next edition of OK! Magazine turn to the section containing photographs of celebrities arriving at the Private Viewing of the V&A's *Bowie Is* exhibition and you find the shot of Noel Gallagher and partner. There heavily cropped out in the background may be my arm or Ana's* head.

We were there because our rice light box *Everyone Born In The United Kingdom: 1947* was commissioned for the exhibition. Noel Gallagher was there because his is Noel Gallagher.

The queue even for the Private View seemed to stretch half way round the block and once inside entry to the exhibition was still on a timed basis, so it was hardly an exclusive gathering but we had a fun time swanning around the V&A amidst the beautiful/beautifully dressed people nibbling genetically shrunk meals in canapé form and sipping the high life. We were a little anxious entering the exhibition as we hadn't seen our piece in its full assembled form but it looked fine. I used a thumb nail to remove the accent on Cafe in our credit plaque and we got on with browsing Bowie memorabilia. People asked if he was going to be there, the answer was clearly no, if he wanted to see any of this stuff he could have nipped up to his loft any time he fancied, why would he travel to London to see it?

*Ana Rutter, who did most of the work on this piece.
James Yarker, 21st March, 2013

Small People With Big Feet
Theater Bonn: Save The World II
Halle Beuel, Bonn Germany
19th - 20th September, 2015

The vast area of the Großer Malersaal (big painters room) provided inspiration for this fifteen minute long piece about climate change. It took a similar approach to scales as *Of All The People In All The World*, its companion piece.

This script was translated and performed in German.

M: Welcome, welcome, please come in but stay behind this blue line. *[audience in position]*
Welcome to the surface of the planet Earth, all 510 million square kilometres of it, represented by the 1,350 square metres of this room.

O: Now, everyone please pick up the blue ribbon, we are going to carry it in a line until I ask you to stop. *[Start to walk]*
From space Earth is seen as a blue planet because 68% of it surface is covered by oceans. Let's stop here, that is 68% of the room. Turn around to take a look at all the beautiful water we have.

M: You may want to step back onto dry land to stop your feet getting wet.
Now if people on that side of the room join Okka Lou by the yellow ribbon and those of you on this side of the room join me with the white ribbon.

O: Great. Now we are going to mark out the world's deserts, lands too dry to sustain human life. So pick up the yellow ribbon and walk it with me *[2.27m from one side wall]*.

M: We are marking out the surface of Earth covered in snow and ice, too cold to sustain human life *[2.14m from the other side wall]*.
These ribbons are not fixed, they have moved around through the Earth's history, they move, but very slowly, 21,000 years ago this line would have been here *[1/3 of the way across]*.
[J&N unroll and position the green ribbon 5m from back wall between yellow and white ribbons]

J: This is all the agricultural land humans use to feed themselves.

O: *[moving to the centre of the unmarked floor area]* Of course, we must add the humans. Gather around everyone, come in. Lovely, stay there, now here we are, standing quite close, one square metre per person. Now, imagine the rest of the world's population is gathering round us, coming in and in, until we're all stood like this, all 7.2 billion of us, one square meter each. *[holding up a cardboard rectangle]* Here we are. All of us. Seven thousand square kilometres of people stood one meter apart. We would all fit on the island of Cyprus *[another cardboard rectangle]*, but we're in Bonn, so I'll rest us all on Germany *[a large cardboard rectangle]*.

M: Okka Lou, let's make this more realistic. We need to spread people out a bit more. 54% of humans live in urban areas now, we should have some cities.
Will you have Tokyo for me, you have London, you have New York, you have Karachi, Mumbai, Shanghai, Seoul, Jakarta.

O: These rectangles are to scale, so let's put them in the right place. All these cities are built on the coast, within 6 meters of sea level, so please place your cities just this side of the blue line. Thank you. So, there we have it, a picture of planet Earth in 2015.

N: 2015! Hold on, we've got a problem! We're not supposed to be doing the ribbons for 2015, we're supposed to be the doing ribbons for 2050.

J: It doesn't matter. 2015 is the same as 2050 isn't it?

N: No, things have changed.

J: Matthias said things happen slowly, what difference does 35 years make?

M: Things used to happen slowly, but that was before we added the humans. Now, since the industrial revolution, things have started to change faster, much faster. The carbon that was locked away under the ground for millions of years is been released into the atmosphere in ever greater quantities.

J: So?

M: So this build up of carbon in the atmosphere, in the form of carbon dioxide, means more heat is being trapped by the Earth's atmosphere rather than escaping out into space. Global temperatures are rising fast, not over thousands of years but in tens of years. So for the year 2050 we have to move the ribbons.

O: Desert team please help me. With a warmer planet the deserts will advance, eating into the agricultural lands, causing a strain on water supplies and an increased chance of drought, forest fires and famine.

M: At the same time as the deserts advance the snow and the ice will retreat.

N: This is good news! There can be more agricultural land.

M: No, these will still be inhospitable places, unsuitable for growing crops. What you must remember is that as the ice melts it flows into the oceans and sea levels rise. We must move the blue ribbon now. Everyone please come and stand by the blue ribbon.

M: We expect in the next 50 years the sea level to rise by 30cm. This extra water will cause higher tides and will start to flood costal areas, with more extreme weather events causing further damage. Rich regions may be able to defend themselves, London for example already has the Thames Barrier, which it already uses but poorer cities and low lying regions will be powerless to stop huge flooding, such as that which affected one million people in Myanmar this summer destroying nearly 5,000 square kilometres of rice crops. Islands like the Maldives will disappear entirely never to be seen again.

O: Wait, wait, wait, wait! I'm not happy about this, are you? Are you? Matthias, do we have to move this ribbon? It's not 2050 yet. Is there anything we can do to not move this ribbon?

M: There is a chance, just a chance, but you need to speak to a friend of mine. Actually, she is a friend of

	us all.
	[J pulls in N who is sitting on a throne of 330 bricks wearing a crown, red velvet cape and waving to the audience]
N:	Good evening everyone. Hello, how are you? I'm pleased to meet you.
O:	Hello, who are you?
N:	I am The Average Citizen Of Germany.
O:	Your throne looks very comfortable!
N:	Yes, these are my carbon emissions for the last 40 days, 1000 kg.
O:	Wow, 1000kg no wonder you are so comfortable.
M:	Speaking of 'comfortable' we should get some other thrones built.
	Sir would you care to be Bangladesh for us? Take 15 bricks and build a throne, next to hers, make yourself comfortable.
	Madam would you care to be Ethiopia for us? Take a couple of bricks and build a throne, next to his. Make yourself comfortable.
	Sir, it's Burundi for you, have a brick. Sit on the end please, enjoy.
O:	Right team I'm afraid we've got this ribbon moving problem going on and to stop it we need to be putting some bricks back in the wheel barrow please. So who's going to help out?
N:	Why are you looking at me!
O:	I think we just thought maybe you'd have some bricks to spare?
N:	Like what? Which ones?
O:	I don't know, can anyone suggest how she could reduce her carbon footprint?
	[the audience makes suggestions N reluctantly agrees to the concessions, bricks are taken off her throne and put back in the barrow]
M:	Okka Lou I've been thinking, it's great that you're putting these bricks back in the barrow but what about our friends here? They're pretty uncomfortable and they're suggesting they'd quite

	like to add some bricks to their seats.
O:	Oh dear, we're already using too many bricks so I don't really want to bring out any more.
M:	But if we don't bring out any more then how are they going to get more comfortable?
	We can help you become more comfortable without needing bricks *[gives Burundi a blow up chair]*.
N:	We can help you become more comfortable without needing brick *[lists things she's given up]*.
	[J pulls on second pallet which has a member of the audience sat on a smaller throne of 260 bricks wearing a cardboard crown].
M:	Hold on, who is this, who's arriving now?
J:	Let me introduce *[audience member's name]* he/she is the Average Citizen of China.
N:	Brilliant he/she can give these people some of his/her bricks.
J:	No, no, no, no, no! Look at all your bricks!
O:	Quiet! It seems that the only fair thing to do is to work out how much carbon we can emit and stay safe, then divide this allocation evenly between us all.

O: Okay, everyone is allowed 90 bricks each for forty days, see it's marked by the hazard tape.
[J puts red and white hazard tape around the Chinese pile]

M: Brilliant! You two hand over your bricks to this lot. Guys does anyone fancy a fridge or a washing machine?

N: What are you joking! I can't give up this lot!

O: It is fair that's the whole point.

J: *[in English]* I'll tell you something that isn't fair. Lots of these bricks don't belong to China, they don't make their citizens comfortable, they are used to make things like iPhones for you lot.

N: What's he saying?

O: He says lots of those bricks should be on your throne because it's carbon on their budget but they use it to build things for you.

N: Well we build loads of cars for you, so you can have these back.
[An alarm goes off on the soundtrack]

M: That's it, times up, we've spent too long arguing. The show is over. We spend a lot of time arguing about all this, about what's right and what's fair but even while we're arguing we need to be doing something. The alarm is sounding and we should all be doing something. We don't need so many bricks on our thrones to be comfortable, we must give some of them up, it's right, it's fair and it's the only thing that will stop the ribbons from moving.
[Room lights out]

O: On July 20th, 1969 two human beings stood on the moon and looked up at the Earth. This is what they saw *[turn light on model Earth]* one whole Earth, no political borders, no thrones, no arguments, no ribbons; a beautiful swirl of white and blue and yellow and green. Let's keep it that way.
[The audience are led out past the model Earth]

Credits
Devised and performed by: Okka Lou Mathis,
Matthias Ruchser & James Yarker
Additional performer: Nuria Catalan
Scenic, lighting and sound design: James Yarker
Administrator: Rowena Wilding
Executive Producer: Roisin Caffrey
Commissioned by: Theatre Bonn for Save the World II

What When
Rheinaue, Bonn
6th - 17th November, 2017

The title What When comes from the familiar chant of protest:

Person with big voice: "What do we want?"
Everyone else: "[insert demand]"
Person with big voice: "When do we want it?"
Everyone else: "[insert deadline for demand*]"

*it is worth noting this deadline is always "now" and never "in a fortnight's time".

When we were asked to submit an idea for Save The World IV to run alongside the World Climate Change Conference (COP23) in Bonn we thought about the demonstrations that surround events such this We were moved by the effort and personal commitment of those who demonstrate and asked ourselves how effective such protests are. We considered how protests often provoke counter-protests and we reflected on how the evolution of mass communication has changed how people demonstrate.

We grew interested in making an installation which would provoke lots of these thoughts and proposed constructing a single protest march that appears to be travelling through time. We were most interested in hand made personal signs and so set about finding images of these. We selected 71 to recreate and added two signs from imaginary future protests. These signs are now placed in an approximate chronological order and for the most part are positioned at a height and angle that reflects how they were being carried when photographed.

Whilst many topics from around the world are covered by this installation, environmental concerns and particularly climate change have been our strongest themes. The second reading of our title "What will happen when?" asks about the future and that is still up for grabs. If enough of us act we help shape this future for the better.

Credits

What When was made by Stan's Cafe
Signs researched, selected, painted and installed by Simon Ford and James Yarker
Sign selection and painting by Craig Stephens
With additional research and painting by Zoe Hemington
Further additional painting by Eve Yarker
Research in Germany by Kathrin Ebmeier
Production support by Laura Killeen
Executive Producer: Roisin Caffrey

We would like to thank the good people of Theater Bonn who commissioned *What When* and for helping us construct it in their workshops.

We would also like to thank, in their absence, everyone whose signs we have recreated for this installation. We hope that were they ever to discover what we have done with their signs that they would be pleased to know that their protest lives on.

We must thank all the friends of Stan's Cafe who responded to an online appeal for photos of protest signs they had seen or made. Thank you for your commitment, we were touched and even if your image didn't get recreated for the installation you inspired us and forced us to think harder about what we were doing.

Finally, we'd like to thank all the photographers whose original photographs captured these signs for us.

About the illustration and design

The illustrations for the covers of these books were undertaken by students at Birmingham City University as the final module of their first-year illustration course during the Spring/Summer of 2018. The images were developed using workshops using variations of the theatre-devising methods produced by Stan's Cafe but adapted and applied to the making of visual work. The resulting work was shown in the pop-up exhibition *The Something Of Somebody Something* at AE Harris in May 2018.

The design concept of the books was produced by final year Graphic Design student Aimee Chapman. These were then further developed for print in a collaborative process between Stan's Cafe and the University's Innovation Product Support Service (IPSS) and involved helping the company with selecting appropriate DTP software, undertaking training and selecting a suitable print on demand service.

Gareth Courage
Lecturer in Illustration
Birmingham City University

www.ingramcontent.com/pod-product-compliance
Lightning Source LLC
Chambersburg PA
CBHW071746080526
44588CB00013B/2166